700029566227

D0996552

CONTRA CROSS

Christopher Robinson

CONTRA CROSS

Insurgency and Tyranny in Central America, 1979-1989

WILLIAM R. MEARA

Naval Institute Press
Annapolis, Maryland

Naval Institute Press
291 Wood Road
Annapolis, MD 21402

Library of Congress Cataloging-in-Publication Data
Meara, William R.
Contra cross: insurgency and tyranny in Central America, 1979—1989 / William R. Meara.
    p. cm.
Includes bibliographical references.
ISBN 1-59114-518-X (alk. paper)
1. Central America—History—1979– 2. Insurgency—Central America. 3. Counterinsurgency—El Salvador—History. 4. Counterrevolutionaries—Nicaragua—History. 5. Military assistance, American—Central America. 6. United States—Military policy. 7. Meara, William R. I. Title.
  F1439.M43 2006
  972.8—dc22

2005037408

Printed in the United States of America on acid-free paper ∞

12 11 10 09 08 07 06   9 8 7 6 5 4 3 2
First printing

All photographs in the gallery are from the author's personal collection.

For my wife, Elisa, who years ago photocopied an early manuscript of this book and carried it home through the hot and noisy streets of Santo Domingo, and has been urging me to get it into print ever since.

HONDURAS

Coco River

Palmerola
Air base

The Bocay

TEGUCIGALPA

Cifuentes

Las
Trojes

Banco
Grande

Danli

Yamales

EL
SALVADOR

Choluteca

Gulf of
Fonseca

NICARAGUA

Lake
Managua

MANAGUA

PACIFIC

Granada

Lake Nicaragua

OCEAN

0   25   50
Miles

COSTA RICA

Christopher Robinson

CONTENTS

PREFACE

I have sworn upon the altar of God, eternal hostility against every form of tyranny over the mind of man.

— Thomas Jefferson to Benjamin Rush, 1800

Now the trumpet summons us again—not as a call to bear arms, though arms we need—not as a call to battle, though embattled we are—but a call to bear the burden of a long twilight struggle year in and year out, "rejoicing in hope, patient in tribulation"—a struggle against the enemies of man: tyranny, poverty, disease and war itself.

— John F. Kennedy, from inaugural address, January 20, 1961

THE HELICOPTER DROPPED DOWN TO TREETOP LEVEL and we began the high-speed run down to the river—down to the border. Fearing Sandinista antiaircraft missiles, the pilot kept the helicopter close to the treetops. Suddenly the river appeared. The pilot spun around and touched down on Banco Grande, a small clearing on the banks of the Coco River. After letting me out, he took off on a supply run. As the helicopter clattered off, the jungle got quiet. I found myself alone with a small group of contras who had that day walked out of Nicaragua.

It was early June 1989 and I was on a mission for the U.S. embassy. I had gone to Banco Grande to interview recently arrived contras. We wanted to find out what was happening across the river in Nicaragua. I had been to this place many times before, but there had always been more people around. This time it was just me and two squads from the Santiago Meza battalion.

My interview with the troops that day didn't produce any really new or noteworthy information. I had heard the same story many times before: Nicaraguan peasants driven to war by the day-to-day absurdities of Marxist Leninism. When asked why they had joined the resistance, this particular bunch spoke about the stupidities of collectivized agriculture. They were especially angry about having to wait in long lines for basic food items that they had previously been able to obtain without difficulty.

But near the end of the interview, something happened that made this visit to Banco Grande very memorable. It had started to rain, and the time for my scheduled extraction was fast approaching. As I shared some candy and idle conversation with the troops, a small group of contra combatants burst through the tree line—this group was heading out of Honduras. They were going back into Nicaragua.

There were five or six of them, and they were hunched over by the weight of enormous rucksacks. They were soaked to the skin by sweat and rain, and were wide-eyed in anticipation of imminent contact with the Sandinistas. These men were about to enter a combat zone, and they moved with the speed and alertness appropriate for such an entry.

For months I had been involved in the larger strategic issues of the Nicaraguan conflict. I had monitored contra reactions to big international events like the Tesoro Beach peace talks and the Bush administration's bipartisan accord on Central America. I had sat in on high-level embassy meetings in which considerations of diplomacy, strategy, and national interest were discussed. And without realizing it I had lost touch with the human element of the war. This visit to Banco Grande brought me back into contact with that human element.

As the patrol trotted across the clearing, I moved to intercept them before they reached the river. I knew it was pointless to try to interview these men—troops going back into Nicaragua were understandably tight-lipped. Besides, I didn't have the heart to squeeze information out of people about to embark on a life-threatening mission. So our encounter was very brief. I shook their hands. I got a little choked up as I wished them good luck. I told them to go with God. They quietly and sincerely thanked me for the good wishes. Then they turned and disappeared into Nicaragua.

I had prided myself on my objectivity about the contras. I had consciously tried not to get emotionally involved. But that day, standing there on the border in the rain with a bunch of young guys who were about to put it all on the line, I found it impossible to stay emotionally detached.

A few weeks later, on July 9, 1989, I said good-bye to Central America. On the plane that carried me out of Honduras I sat next to Comandante Franklyn, the senior military leader of the Nicaraguan democratic resistance—the chief of the contras.[1] As the plane cruised over the Gulf of Mexico, we reminisced about the previous year. During lapses in the conversation I thought back on other chapters in my ten years of involvement in Central America.

I first went to the region in 1979 as a volunteer English teacher working at a Catholic mission school. Ten years later I was a U.S. embassy liaison officer to the Nicaraguan contras. As a student I had bounced around Central America with a backpack and had visited Sandinista Nicaragua. As an army officer I had participated in the big anti-Sandinista military maneuvers in Honduras, served in El Salvador as one of the fifty-five U.S. military advisers there, and worked on the staff of the U.S. Southern Command in Panama. In the Foreign Service I had been special assistant to the U.S. ambassador in Tegucigalpa. The decade had taken me across the region and across the spectrum of opinion on our controversial Central America policy. I had seen insurgencies from both sides: in El Salvador, we were putting one down; in Nicaragua, we were propping one up. This book is a look back at that decade.

An M-16 rifle cartridge sits on a bookshelf in my living room. The powder has been removed, and the shell has been fashioned into a crucifix. This is a contra cross, the symbol of the Nicaraguan anti-Communist resistance. While the war in Nicaragua was only one part of the broader, region-wide struggle I describe in this book, *Contra Cross* is an appropriate title. This bullet-cross captures the mix of ideology, theology, idealism, and brutal violence that characterized Central America during the 1980s. And these two simple words, *contra cross*, seem to embrace much of what went on in those difficult years: this was a struggle against something—against Communism. The struggle was a burden, a cross carried by the Central Americans who fought it. Regrettably, these two words also capture something of the treachery that seemed to lurk in the jungle foliage during the last months of the conflict.

Most of the other books about the decade of violence in Central America have been written either by former officials who focus on the bureaucratic battles in Washington or by journalists who write from the position of adversarial outsiders. A variety of professional restraints and prohibitions prevent many U.S. government insiders who worked in the field from writing about their experiences. Of course, I don't pretend to speak for anyone else—I am simply offering the view of one insider who worked in the region and had good vantage points from which to observe the conflict.

I wrote this book because I think the public could benefit from knowing what it was like on the ground, implementing U.S. policy in Central America during the 1980s. A lot of bad feelings linger in the United States about what we did in that region during the Reagan years. I don't share these feelings. I am proud of what we did and what we tried to do. I hope this book helps to alleviate any angst about Central America that may linger in the hearts of concerned Americans.

I don't pretend to have seen it all. For example, I had no contact with the infamous Iran-contra scandal. But I am one of the very few Americans who worked on both the Nicaraguan contra insurgency and the Salvadoran counterinsurgency. I hope that by describing my experiences in these conflicts I will shed some light on the kinds of problems and challenges that the United States faces when it tries to deal with insurgencies in foreign lands.

In conventional war, mountain ranges and rivers are key terrain features. But when we get involved in foreign insurgencies culture quickly becomes the key feature, the equivalent of a mountain range that cannot be ignored. In El Salvador, I found out the hard way that sometimes soldiers from a different culture don't think like we do. I also came to the conclusion that we Americans are not very good at understanding cultural differences, even when dealing with cultures that are relatively close to our own. I hope my trials and tribulations in this area will prove illuminating.

If the United States is to be able to deal effectively with insurgency, personnel with language skills are absolutely essential. I'm not talking about the kind of skill that comes from a six-month course. I mean a level of fluency that allows a person to sit by a campfire with guerrillas and tell jokes (jokes that will *really* make them laugh) in their language. During my ten years in Central America I gradually went from making frequent and embarrassing (and in some cases truly appalling) linguistic errors to being able to "curse like a contra." I hope this book makes clear how important language skills really are.

The United States has the world's most powerful military, but that does not necessarily mean that we are good at dealing with insurgency and guerrilla warfare. I found that our proficiency at high-intensity military operations actually hindered our ability to deal with insurgency. Our tanks and our bombers seemed to make us smug and overconfident. And our military officers often seemed to scorn the touchy-feely cultural-linguistic skills needed in what they tellingly refer to as "small wars" or "low-intensity conflict." As an army officer involved in the ethereal battle for Central American hearts and minds, I frequently found myself crashing up against the rigidities of a military organization designed to deal with large-scale conflict.

America's deficiencies in this area are not limited to our military. In Central America I found that shortcomings were government-wide: Why was the support that the Communists provided to the Salvadoran guerrillas so much more effective than the support the U.S. government gave to the contra guerrillas of Nicaragua? I hope this book sheds some light on why we are not well prepared to deal with insurgency and guerrilla war.

Working on insurgency often means working with or through foreign forces. Surrogate warfare has many advantages, but it also involves complex issues:

What kind of emotional distance should you maintain from your foreign allies, from people who are risking their lives for a cause?

What do you do when you discover that your surrogates are violating human rights?

What happens when the United States wants to call it quits but our foreign partners want to fight on?

How much loyalty do we owe to people who have fought for us?

How should our national values and heritage affect our interaction with foreign guerrilla allies?

We faced all of these issues in Central America. I hope this description of my experiences will be of use to those who face similar challenges in the future.

This is not a kiss-and-tell book. I reveal no classified information, and I hope that I betray no confidences. In Central America I worked closely with people who operate in secrecy. They trusted me, and I will not violate that trust. With the exception of one case from the history books, this book contains no mention of those who worked in a clandestine mode. The manuscript was reviewed by the U.S. Department of State to ensure that it reveals no classified information. The exclusion of classified material was not an impediment; nothing really significant had to be left out, and readers should not think that the real story lies buried somewhere in secret files. The opinions expressed in this book are my own and do not necessarily reflect those of the U.S. government.

I have deliberately obscured the identities of many of the Central Americans and of some of the North Americans; many are referred to by false names. When I first wrote the book, the war was not yet completely over and I didn't want to put anyone in danger. I have retained some of the pseudonyms because I'm not sure whether these people would be comfortable with public discussion of their wartime activities.

I wrote most of this book in Tegucigalpa, Honduras, during 1989, and in Bilbao, Spain, during 1990. The world has changed quite a bit since then—I ask readers to remember that the Cold War was still under way during the period described, and was just starting to end as I was writing.

Finally, while this book deals with a very serious topic, many funny and pleasant things happened to me during my time as a policy implementer in Central America. I don't think that I was in any way traumatized by my experiences in the region, and I will not try to dramatize this book by feigning such trauma. Levity laced our days in Central America. It was part of life there, and it has a place here as well.

CHAPTER 1
GUATEMALA

As the rich waltzed in expensive rags
poor Indians watched through a ground floor window
brown faces pressed to the glass
Soldiers' machine guns discouraged gate crashers.
Micro-cosmic Guatemala!

ON THE FLIGHT FROM MIAMI TO GUATEMALA CITY I started to worry. This was my first trip outside the United States. I was twenty years old, traveling alone, and had only a vague notion of where I was going and what I would be doing. My Spanish professor at Manhattan College had invited me to spend my sophomore summer "working at a mission school in Guatemala." There would be no pay, but all of my expenses would be taken care of. I would be working with a small group of students from our college (none of whom I had met).

Although I was majoring in Latin American studies, I still had to look in the atlas to refresh my memory on Guatemala. I had very rudimentary high school Spanish (straight Cs)—I couldn't even pronounce the name of the town I would be living in. As I flew south I wondered what I would be doing at the school—I worried that they might make me a janitor or a gardener or something like that.

I arrived in Guatemala wearing the standard attire of an American college student: jeans, sneakers, and a T-shirt. The immigration official introduced me to the correct pronunciation of my destination: it was *Way-way-ten-AN-go* (*Way-way* for short), not *Hoo-ee-Hoo-ee-ten-ango*.

I was relieved when my professor, Brother Peter Stewart, appeared out of the crowd. Brother Peter explained that Huehuetenango is a mountain town northwest of Guatemala City, and he briefed me on what I would be doing: teaching (not sweeping). That was good news, but now I had a new worry: had I signed up to spend my twentieth summer in a mountain monastery with a bunch of monks?

After one day in the capital, we boarded a bus for the five-hour trip to Huehue. Many Americans seem to think of Latin America as a vast extension of a big-city U.S. Hispanic barrio—not very interesting, not very exotic, not even really foreign. Guatemala is one of the best places in the hemisphere to shatter these stereotypes. On the bus ride to Huehue I discovered the exotic, profoundly foreign beauty of Guatemala. As we wound through the brilliantly green mountains, we shared the bus with a group of Guatemala's Indians. Dressed in their colorful, intricately woven clothing, the Indians spoke quietly in a language that sounded like something from far-off Asia.

Guatemala was also a good place to begin an exploration of the ideological issues of Cold War Central America. In 1954, Guatemala's leftist government was overthrown with the help of the United States. Twenty-five years later, many on the left seemed to regard this coup as the root of all evil in the region. During the decade ahead I would find myself struggling with many of the issues raised by the 1954 coup, and would cross paths with one of those responsible for it.

When the bus finally entered Huehue, Peter asked the driver to let us off at the entrance of the De la Salle School. My doubts about the entire endeavor intensified as we struggled with our bags on the dusty street corner. Then Peter opened the gate to the school's grounds and we entered a lush, beautifully landscaped compound. Looking up to the balcony of the Spanish colonial–style Brothers' House, I saw for the first time the other members of the summer teaching team: a group of seven very amiable students from Manhattan College. My worries about a boring summer among the monks diminished. It looked like this was going to be fun. Little did I know that it would be the start of ten years of almost continuous involvement in Central America.

I quickly settled in as a boarder in the home of a nice Guatemalan family. The very serious man of the house explained that no English would be spoken under his roof—the Brothers were paying him to feed and house me, but they were also paying him to make sure that I learned Spanish. He told me (only half-facetiously) that if I didn't want to die of hunger I should learn Spanish . . . *pronto*!

At the school, I learned that I would be teaching basic English grammar to junior high school kids. We worked at the Christian Brothers' Colegio de la Salle boys' school and at an adjacent girls' school run by the Sisters of the Sacred Family—a charming group of high-spirited European nuns.

It was a great summer for all the American volunteers. Working with our students and living with our families, we learned about Guatemala. Our classes reflected the ethnic diversity of the Guatemalan highlands. Fifty percent of Guatemala's population consists of Indians like those I had met on the bus. These people live in a world apart from Hispanic "Ladino" Guatemala. They are the victims of poverty and discrimination. They are also the heirs to the fascinating culture of the Mayas.

Huehuetenango itself provided an ideal setting for a first summer abroad. With a population of about ten thousand, set amidst the stunning Cuchumatanes Mountains, Huehue was a friendly place that opened its arms to a group of enthusiastic—if not culturally sensitive—young gringos. We quickly became minor celebrities on the Huehue social scene. A visit to the central park inevitably resulted in meetings with students who wanted to chat with their *maestros*.

We had a lot of fun. Our afternoons were spent at a beautiful and completely incongruous swimming pool (complete with poolside bar). We were less than completely serious missionaries. Sipping a cool drink at poolside, a team member would sigh and remark, "Life is tough in the missions!" or, "I wonder what the poor people are doing today?" In the evenings we all got together for dinner, followed by visits to Huehue's not-so-hopping but culturally interesting cantinas.

We were also less than completely serious teachers. We were only a few years older than some of our students, and there was some tomfoolery in the classrooms. Every schoolroom in the world has its class clown, and our Guatemalan classrooms were no exception. One of the other guys on the team and I got into a little trouble when we retaliated against the class clowns by teaching them erroneous (and we thought humorous) translations for their Indian names. Brother Peter was horrified when one of my charges met us on the town square and proudly announced that she had learned to say her name in English: "Pain-in-the-Neck." But, hey, her pronunciation was perfect! I hope our antics didn't drive anyone into the ranks of the guerrillas.

Huehue was calm in the summer of 1979, but there were rumblings over the horizon. Nicaragua was already in flames; Sandinista rebels were about to overthrow the Somoza dictatorship. We followed the war with great interest. We watched journalist Bill Stewart being killed on television by Nicaraguan National Guardsmen in Managua. It all seemed very far away, but we were soon to discover that many of the forces that were at work in Nicaragua were also present in tranquil Huehue.

Working with Catholic missionaries put me in contact with liberation theology. Loosely defined as a position of advocacy for the poor, liberation theology had its roots in the changes carried out by the Church in the 1960s. Moderate liberation theologians called for the church to speak out against social injustice and to work from the pulpit for a more just society. Radical liberation theologians encouraged a much more active role, sometimes interpreting the call for advocacy as a call for revolution, a call for the complete destruction of the existing social order. A very small number of Church people became members of Marxist-Leninist guerrilla groups.

The religious community in which I was sojourning had no guerrillas, but its members had a broad range of interpretations about the proper role of the Church. Some of the younger members were inspired by the prominent role of the clergy in the unfolding Sandinista victory. All were understandably frustrated with the corrupt and brutal dictatorship of Guatemala's General Lucas García. Youthful impatience, sympathy for the poor, a desire for a quick solution, and an exposure to dependency economic theory (the theory that Latin poverty and American prosperity were both the direct results of U.S. economic exploitation) combined to make many members of our community at least a little sympathetic to those pushing for radical solutions. Most repudiated the use of violence, but there were those who could justify the need to take up arms.

I had majored in Latin American studies and economics in the hope that I would someday be able to do something about Latin America's poverty. Conditions in Guatemala were appalling, and I thought that radical options were worthy of consideration. I too was suffering a bit from exposure to dependency theory and sometimes wondered if the Guatemalans were poor because we were rich. But I also had some doubts about the coming revolution. "What about the Cubans?" I asked. "Aren't there Cubans out there with the guerrillas? Aren't the Cubans calling the shots?" I was told that there was no evidence of outside Communist involvement, but I remained skeptical.

I was working with bright, well-educated people, but their level of political naïveté and wishful thinking was quite high. Some of these people seemed wedded to the romantic notion of a heroic national revolution of desperate *campesinos* reluctantly driven to violence by the repressive political economy of Guatemala. There was no room in this dream for the reality of cynical foreign Communist manipulators who pulled revolutionary strings for their own geopolitical purposes. It was far easier to ignore that disturbing reality.

During the summer of 1979, the only real sign of trouble in Huehue was the writing on the walls: "Lucas y Somoza son la misma cosa!" (Lucas and Somoza are the same thing!) When I returned to work in the school the following summer, the situation had worsened noticeably. Military patrols were present and the climate was much more tense; the second summer in Guatemala was not nearly as pleasant as the first.

I graduated from college in 1981, right into the middle of a recession and a federal government hiring freeze. I had been hoping to get a job with one of the federal government's foreign affairs agencies. Disappointed, I decided to be patient and wait until something of interest opened up.

During this frustrating period of unsuccessful job searching, I periodically managed to scrape together enough money for trips to Latin America; I had a lot of energy and a thirst for foreign adventure. Some of these trips were risky, but they sustained my interest in the region through an otherwise discouraging period of unemployment. I learned a lot, and I developed some Central America "street smarts" that would prove useful in the years ahead.

By this time, the violence that was tearing through Central America was no longer bypassing Huehuetenango. Communist guerrillas discovered that the injustices suffered by the Guatemalan Indians provided fertile ground for revolution. Right-wing thugs were reacting with indiscriminate violence. During the period that I was traveling around the region, the death squads paid a call on our little community.

In January 1982, I flew to Mexico City and began a bus trip south to Guatemala. After about a week of bouncing through southern Mexico, I finally crossed the Guatemalan border and made my way down to Huehue. I found the little town noticeably tense—it was definitely not the happy mountain town I remembered. I hung around for a few days before heading on to Guatemala City.

On February 13, 1982 (about two weeks after I departed), Brother Jim Miller, an American missionary from Wisconsin, was assassinated in Huehuetenango. Jim worked at the dormitory that the Christian Brothers ran for Indian kids. Apparently, educating Indians had become a subversive act in the eyes of the

Guatemalan radical right. I didn't know Jim very well. He had arrived in Huehue at the tail end of my 1980 summer visit. But for the first time, someone I knew had been killed by the violence in Central America. I was outraged by the killing and launched a letter-writing campaign directed at my congressional representatives and the Department of State (my future employer). I also vented steam at Central America protest rallies in New York City.

While Jim Miller's killers were never brought to justice, concern about human rights violations eventually led the U.S. government to cut off assistance to Guatemala and to increase the pressure for change. The military government that had presided over the wave of violence that claimed Jim Miller's life was overthrown and eventually replaced by a civilian government. I like to think that concerned Americans who spoke out against human rights violations in Guatemala contributed to this change.

For many Americans, their first trip abroad is the first time they become aware of their American culture; for the first time, they realize that they carry their own distinctive cultural characteristics. I made this discovery in Huehue. While I had been through numerous college courses in which cultural differences were discussed, these lessons didn't start to sink in until I confronted their practical, day-to-day manifestations in Guatemala. This initial exposure to the reality of cultural difference was, for me, the most important educational experience of those two Guatemalan summers.

My experience in Guatemala was long enough and intense enough to take me beyond some of the silly conclusions about foreign cultures that many American tourists carry home with them. Some American travelers tend to idealize foreign cultures, and to disparage their own. Some have the rather cozy and simplistic notion that "the foreigners are OK, but we're messed up!" My brief but intense exposure to Guatemalan culture was enough to disabuse me of this idea; I think the entire group of student volunteers left Guatemala with the understanding that every culture — including our own — has positive and negative features. For example, we all were impressed by the warmth and the sense of community engendered by the extended family structure, but we were shocked by the coldness with which these families treated the very young Indian girls who worked for them as household servants. I became genuinely fond of Guatemala, but at the same time I became aware of some of the ugly features of the culture, and of the culturally based problems that bedevil the country and the region.[1]

CHAPTER 2
VISITING THE SANDINISTAS

"I will allow you to come for the conference you want and I also allow you to come with a guard of 500 men." And when "you come to my mountains," Sandino advised, "make your wills beforehand." Until then, the general concluded, "I remain your most obedient servant, who ardently desires to put you in a handsome tomb with beautiful bouquets of flowers."

"Bravo! General," Hatfield replied. "If words were bullets and phrases were soldiers, you would be a field marshal instead of a mule thief."

— 1927 correspondence between Augusto César
Sandino and Capt. G. D. Hatfield, USMC, as
recounted in *The Sandino Affair* by Neill Macaulay

WHEN I FINISHED COLLEGE IN 1981 it was fashionable for graduates to embark on a grand tour of Europe. But London and Paris seemed very tame—I wanted to see Sandinista Nicaragua. I was looking for adventure and intrigue, and I had a lot of curiosity about the big Sandinista experiment. I hadn't yet made up my mind about Sandinismo; I wanted to see it for myself. Getting there was simple: I bought my plane tickets from a travel agent, I went to the Nicaraguan consulate in New York to pick up a visa, I loaded my backpack, and I was off.

When I arrived in Managua in May 1981, the Sandinistas had been in power less than two years. At first, I did not get the impression that I had entered a totalitarian police state. I was not part of any official tour, and no one attempted to control my movements. I had no specific plans for touring the country, so I just began wandering around the capital.

Like many visitors, I rather stupidly asked the cab driver to take me downtown, only to discover that there wasn't much town there. A 1972 earthquake had destroyed most of the buildings. I could see where the city blocks had been, but most of them were completely vacant, and grass grew over much of the area. Ten years after the earthquake, the useless shells of old office buildings rose from strange urban grasslands. Burned-out armored cars—remnants of the fight against Somoza—littered the landscape.

At what remained of the Central Park square, I found the facade of the old cathedral covered with a huge image of Augusto César Sandino, Nicaragua's nationalist hero. Banners proclaiming the virtues of Marxist Leninism were everywhere. The tomb of revolutionary leader Carlos Fonseca Amador had been installed adjacent to the central square.

On the first day I just wandered around snapping pictures. People were quite friendly. Outside the national palace a teenager asked if he could practice his English. We spoke for a while—he complained that there weren't many American visitors anymore. He said that his family was going to a concert at the Rubén Darío Theater that evening and asked if I would like to go along; a countryman of mine would be singing . . . someone named Joan Baez.

The Cuban Ballet Folklorico opened the show. Ms. Baez sang a rather strange combination of old U.S. civil rights ballads and current pop hits. (I remember trying to figure out why she had selected "Don't Cry for Me Argentina.") Some of the Sandinista leaders were there. After the show I was asked if I would like to go backstage to meet the star.

My escorts lied and told the Sandinista guards that I was an old friend of Joan's from the United States. I soon found myself at a little after-the-show gathering in Joan Baez's dressing room. Joan greeted me warmly; she was very upbeat and seemed enthusiastic about the Sandinista revolution. After chatting with her for a few minutes, I noticed a tall American hovering nearby. Finally he stuck out his hand and introduced himself as the U.S. ambassador—it was Ambassador Lawrence Pezzulo. This was all on my first night in Nicaragua.

The next morning I took a twenty-five-cent train ride (on an open-air car) down to Granada and Lake Nicaragua. I rented a boat and toured the lake's beautiful tropical islands. "Why do the islands all have swimming pools?" I asked my guide.

"Because, señor, the lake is filled with sharks."

"Why didn't you tell me?" (as I removed my feet from the water).

"You didn't ask."

I roamed freely around the country and spoke to a lot of ordinary people. And gradually I became disillusioned with the great Sandinista experiment.

Shortly after I got back to the States, I wrote a short article that captures my youthful reactions to 1981 Nicaragua:

Managua had a surreal, seductive flavor, a quality that fueled my sympathy for her inhabitants.

Sandino's image shimmered over what remained of the city's skyline. Outlined in golden lights on the south face of the only still-standing high-rise, framed by volcano and lake, the rebel's figure dominated Managua's vista.

I gazed down from the steps of the Intercontinental Hotel. The hour was filled with both sunset and wild lightning, but it was the confident figure of Augusto César Sandino that turned the twilight electric.

The sweet aroma of a wood fire drifted in the cool, storm-blown breeze. As lightning hit the volcano, I slung the camera over my shoulder and stepped into the Nicaraguan dusk. I was a tourist searching for that rarest of Central American attractions: hope.

Across the street from the hotel, teenaged Sandinistas congregated around guard posts, sharing cigarettes and quiet talk with comrades on duty. Pique must have mixed with tactical considerations when these kids turned Anastasio Somoza's bunker into their downtown garrison.

On the perimeter, the heirs of Sandino met girlfriends, sipped Pepsi, and lazily watched the storm that moved across the lake with nightfall. The BeeGees serenaded the scene from a distant stereo. Chicas-Bonitas-Sandinistas strolled by in tight-fitting fatigues; beautiful girls with big dark eyes (and small Czech submachine guns). While their contemporaries in my country tossed Frisbees and polished Chevies, young Nicas cleaned rifles and polished ideology.

At the concert, Joan Baez and an emotionally charged audience sang revolutionary ballads. When they sang about a young rebel killed in action, many in the audience had tears in their eyes.

Afterward, as I sped through Managua on a Nicaraguan's Yamaha, I assessed the revolution.

I thought that reality had lived up to my hopes and expectations. I had been in Guatemala during the Nicaraguan Civil War. From our mountain village in the western highlands, my friends and I had cheered the Sandinistas' victory. They had defeated repression similar to that which we were witnessing. Machine-gunned convents, tortured students, assassinated priests; the carnage of Guatemala was fertile soil for the seeds of revolutionary sympathy. I became biased in favor of the Sandinistas and I carried this prejudice with me to Nicaragua. At the close of my first day in Managua I felt that my sympathy had been justified.

There is a park in Managua, the Luis A. Velazquez Park. Named for a child killed in the struggle against Somoza, it has a shaded concession stand, a jukebox, and on good days, a pleasant breeze. Swarms of kids keep the music playing, foreign travelers drop by to compare notes, and the soldiers there are more interested in the girls than they are in hassling the gringos. I sat there for several afternoons, talking with people, reading the local tabloids . . . and slowly growing disillusioned with Nicaragua's Sandinista revolution.

During my first day in Managua, like a yokel on his first trip to the city, I had seen only the glitter—the bright lights of the great social experiment. It took a few days on the street to shatter my rose-colored glasses and to show me that I would not, despite hope and expectation, find my quarry in Nicaragua.

I had hoped to find pluralism or at least its seeds. Instead I found one group steadily taking control of many aspects of Nicaraguan life. In place of the promised respect for free expression, I found people intimidated into silent conformity, a courageous opposition newspaper seemingly doomed to government shutdown. Where I looked for a nationalist revolution, I found the hallmarks of Soviet manipulation.

I cared about the future of Central America, and I did not want to see these things. I wanted to see only the glitter, the signs of hope and potential progress. But as an American student I had been trained to scrutinize, and when I took a close look at the Sandinistas, I was forced to recognize the repressive, totalitarian quality of the new regime.

Being there had made the difference—I prepared to leave Nicaragua with a drastically changed opinion of the revolution. As I sat in the park, I thought about how different Sandinista Nicaragua appeared when viewed from elsewhere. I hadn't really had any startling revelations in Nicaragua, but I returned home with opinions that I would have scoffed at a month earlier. I concluded that this change of heart was the result of the change in venue—the change in vantage point.

From New York, revolution seemed romantic, and Communism chimerical. The Sandinistas had a radical chic image—a rock album was named for them. Up close, the revolution lost much of its romance. Communism became less of a right-wing fantasy when the comrade with the Kalashnikov rifle demanded to see my papers.

And it had all looked so different from Guatemala. I remembered how it had looked from there when I spoke to a young Guatemalan nun. At A. C. Sandino airport, Sister and I spoke quietly of Nicaragua, and of some mutual friends in Guatemala. I found that I had a lot in common with the young nun. When I had lived in her country, I had shared many of her political views. But now we disagreed. A visit to Nicaragua had reinforced her support for the revolution, but it had turned me away from the Sandinistas' radical option.

Numbed by the atrocities of Guatemala's right-wing regime, she mistook the absence of these horrors for liberty. She overlooked the subtle psychological atrocity of the totalitarian state. Our destinations were our homelands and our assessments were clearly influenced by these destinations—she was going to Guatemala from Nicaragua Libre; I was bound for the United States from Communist Nicaragua.

They announced my flight and the nun asked me to pray for Guatemala. I asked her to keep Nicaragua in her prayers.

Havana sparkled under the crescent moon. Seconds later the Keys pointed the way to Miami.

New York Times editor A. M. Rosenthall visited Managua in the early 1980s and came up with the most succinct description of Sandinista Nicaragua I have ever heard. He called it "Poland with palm trees."

When I was in Nicaragua, there was some rumbling in the hills: people spoke quietly and cautiously of ambushes and the mysterious activities of armed groups in the northern provinces. I didn't pay much attention. I didn't know that in the years ahead I would become very closely involved with these armed groups, with the people who were launching the ambushes.

CHAPTER 3
IN THE GREEN MACHINE

*To fight and conquer in all your battles is not supreme excellence;
supreme excellence consists in breaking the enemy's resistance
without fighting. . . . Nor is it the acme of excellence if you fight and
conquer and the whole empire says, "Well done!" True excellence
is to plan secretly, to move surreptitiously, to foil the enemy's
intentions and balk his schemes, so that at last, the day may be won
without shedding a drop of blood.*

—*The Art of War* by Sun Tzu (circa 500 BC)

I HAD GRADUATED IN THE MIDDLE OF A SEVERE RECESSION, but luckily I had
a military connection that allowed me to keep body and soul together, and
kept me occupied between overseas explorations. When I was seventeen I had
joined a local National Guard unit. After high school, the Guard had sent me
off for a year of active duty in the army. I remained active in the National Guard
throughout college. During the long summer vacation after my freshman year I
went through Officer Candidate School (OCS) at Fort Benning, Georgia.

I was nineteen when I went to OCS; it was a very formative experience. It
was 1978, and most of our instructors had been in Vietnam. Their bitter experiences brought a real sense of urgency to the instruction. Under the hot Georgia
sun, with a platoon of fellow students standing in formation behind that day's

student platoon leader, the instructors would swarm on their victim. "Status!" they would bark. "Account for your troops! Where are they?" That day's leader was expected to be able to provide an instantaneous account of all his charges. If he appeared rattled or uncertain, the pressure was increased. One of the instructors would start making helicopter noises. "Have you got them all? Are they all here? Can we lift off? Give me a decision, Candidate!" The poor candidate who erred in this kind of test was told (with scorn that obviously came from bitter memories) that he had just left one of his soldiers in the jungle with the Viet Cong. They wanted us to internalize the army's core leadership values—a sense of duty, dedication to the accomplishment of the mission, and a profound sense of personal responsibility for the American soldiers placed in our charge.

As the end of each college year approached, I would start consulting the army's course catalogs in search of military courses that would fit in with my academic schedule. The army has a lot of schools, so I was usually able to find suitable courses.

Several of these training tours took me to Fort Bragg, North Carolina. The bachelor officers' quarters (BOQ) at Fort Bragg are adjacent to the John F. Kennedy Special Warfare Center, the academic home of the U.S. Army Special Forces—the famed Green Berets. In my off-duty hours at Bragg I visited the Special Warfare Center, and there I found an organization that seemed to come straight out of a James Bond movie. While the rest of the army seemed bogged down in boring and repetitive preparations for an unlikely conventional war in Europe, Special Forces was all about derring-do in unconventional battles in exotic Third World locations. While the rest of the army prepared soldiers to serve as little cogs in a gigantic and stifling war machine, "SF" wanted small teams to be ready to parachute clandestinely behind enemy lines to link up with indigenous guerrillas.

Perhaps my interest in Special Forces resulted from two movies I had seen as a kid: *Lawrence of Arabia* (T. E. Lawrence was the quintessential SF adviser) and *The Green Berets* (a film that has almost religious significance at Fort Bragg). Special Forces impressed me as a group of intellectual adventurers who valued not only the military skills needed to operate in hostile foreign areas, but also the linguistic and intercultural skills needed to accomplish the mission. I had discovered a subculture of the U.S. Army that seemed to be exactly what I was looking for. I completed the prerequisite airborne (parachute) training in 1982 and was soon on my way to the six-month Special Forces Qualification Course—the "Q course."

It was a good time to go to the Special Forces course. The Reagan administration had made revitalization of the Special Operations Forces a priority. Guerrilla wars raged from Afghanistan to Angola to El Salvador, and we watched alumni of the course depart for confidential missions in distant lands.

The officers in my class formed an interesting fraternity. We had a medical doctor, a dentist, a veterinarian, and a helicopter pilot. We had five or six officers from foreign armies: Singapore, Egypt, Israel, Malawi, and Indonesia were represented. These foreigners were fully integrated into the class—they participated in everything except a few classified lectures. Each allied officer had an American sponsor who was tasked with helping him along. I was the sponsor for a very capable captain from Singapore, Ng Ee Peng. He ended up helping me more than I helped him. "NG" was a very tough soldier, and he seemed to take SF school in stride. While the rest of us were hanging on by our fingertips, he somehow found the time and energy for some extracurricular study. In an effort to perfect his English, during the course he read an entire pocket dictionary, entry by entry, questioning me about usage and nuance, and making note of the lessons learned.

The difficult course forged strong bonds. It was one of the few times in my army career that I felt like a member of a "band of brothers." The Q course began with the "Basic Skills" phase—a grueling, one-month visit to the Special Forces training base at Camp Mackall, North Carolina. The curriculum focused on land navigation, survival, and patrolling—the basic skills needed to survive as a member of a small team operating behind enemy lines. For one month we struggled and suffered together. By the time we left Camp Mackall we were a close-knit group.

I had some time on my hands after I graduated from Special Forces school, so I wrote a few short articles about the experience. An excerpt from one of them may help convey what the training was like:

On the last day of the first phase of Army Special Forces training, we still had numerous opportunities to fail. A mistake on the jump, a bad gust of wind—there are at least a hundred ways to get hurt jumping, all of them easy to do, with most involving painful injuries to the back or the lower extremities. With a mandatory twelve-mile march starting on the drop zone, a twisted ankle meant painful failure. Of the 305 guys who had started with us one month earlier, only 131 had made it to this, the final hurdle. The standards were clear, victory was in sight.

All that remained of the dreaded Phase 1 was a one-thousand-foot combat equipment parachute jump from a C-130 Hercules followed by a twelve-mile march with a forty-five-pound pack. One thousand feet. Twelve miles. Forty-five pounds. Three hours . . . but it's not over till the fat lady sings.

As I sat next to the runway waiting for the aircraft, I fought the cold wind in a struggle for high spirits. I was pinned down by my parachute and rucksack, and the wind beat against the back of my neck. I ate a C-ration. There were abortive attempts at song, but the wind and the cold squelched that. There was no denying it; we were very cold.

Waiting is the worst part of military parachute jumping. After you go through all the contortions necessary to get your equipment on, all you want to do is get it over with. Paratroopers get very sullen when they are waiting to jump. Afterward there is a lot of euphoric yelling and backslapping, but before the jump most guys are alone with their thoughts.

They put fifteen of us out of the airplane in seventeen seconds. I was number twelve, so I was in the aircraft long enough to hear the involuntary, visceral screaming that takes place when guys are rushing for the door.

"Go! Go! Go!" Then a blast of wind, light, and noise. Military parachuting is a little like jumping into a pool from a high diving board—there is a rush of wind and a blur of rapid movement followed by a crash, rapid deceleration, then silence. My parachute opened and I turned into the wind. This maneuver always reminded me of seagulls facing into the wind to hang suspended in space. As the horizon came up, I heard myself whimper and I felt my body tense in anticipation of the landing shock. It always required a conscious effort for me to relax my leg muscles before impact.

On the ground, I gathered up my gear while breathing short, fast breaths. It had been a good one. I felt strong, euphoric. I'd forgotten the cold, and I was elated about not being injured. The aircraft passed overhead again, and I watched the last group come out. Gradually sensation returned and the adrenaline rush faded. I became human again.

I thought the twelve-miler would start like many of the 10K races that I've seen: with a lot of unrealistic, overambitious sprinting followed by early burnout. I'd misjudged my colleagues. When the clock struck five, our class moved out with enthusiastic but prudent haste. We'd learned well the limits that a forty-five-pound pack places on a man. In countless marches during our month at the Special Forces training camp, we'd all at one time or another reached our personal limits; forty-five pounds brings the marathoner's wall a lot closer to the starting line.

As night fell on the pines, the field spread out and the race began to take on its unique character. There was a lot at stake. Careers were on the line. Failure meant another agonizing month at Camp Mackall. We were in stiff competition, but not with each other. We were fighting ourselves and competing with time. There was very limited illumination on the night of the march; moonlight through the clouds left just enough light for us to see the contrast between the sand trails and the dark forest. Storming through these dark corridors, classmates appeared as indistinguishable dark specters.

At five miles I heard the voice of my team leader, Capt. Steven Overton. Steve had been one of the toughest guys in the class; I was reassured to find myself keeping up with him. We exchanged some gallows humor, and I was able to pass him a small piece of C-ration chocolate. Food had been scarce at Camp Mackall, and I'll never be able to repay Steve for all the food he had given me when I was in short supply. We both knew this, and we laughed at the puniness of the small chunk of candy that I passed to him in the night. It's the thought that counts.

Two hours and thirty-five minutes into the march, with approximately two-thirds of the class behind me, I realized that the end was approaching and that success was likely. Earlier marches had pushed me to my limit—to the point of seeing stars on hot, bright afternoons—but as we approached the finish I felt strong and confident. It was like running through blackened suburban streets on cool summer nights, with feet and street invisible, and movement noted mainly by the wind in the runner's face. I was going to make it.

The march and Phase 1 ended at a point on the road about a quarter mile from Camp Mackall's perimeter. Slowly, with steam rising from our bodies, we walked that last leg in small, quiet groups. I heard the fat lady singing.

Guerrilla University

Phase 2 was the academic portion of the course. In contrast to the austere environment of Camp Mackall, Phase 2 had us living in comfort in the Fort Bragg BOQ, working on essentially a nine-to-five, Monday-through-Friday schedule. Here we learned the theory and doctrine behind the Special Forces' mission. We focused on the primary SF responsibility: unconventional warfare.

Many outsiders think of the Special Forces as commandos—ninja warrior door-kickers who blacken their faces and sneak behind enemy lines to take out something or someone strategically important. But in reality the main job of Special Forces is training, advising, and assisting foreign guerrillas, or "Gs." Its primary mission is surrogate guerrilla warfare.

Phase 2 was like being enrolled in a very bizarre university: we majored in guerrilla war. It was fun and easy. We went to lectures and wrote term papers. To stay in practice we occasionally went out on a night parachute jump. (A reminder of the difference between SF and the rest of the army: One of our instructors once paused and said solemnly, "Gentleman, one very important thing about preparation for SF airborne operations: always bring something to read." We always did.) We learned how to train our Gs to blow things up. We made a field trip to a nearby port facility and spent the day touring the harbor, trying to figure out the best way to destroy it.

The instructors frequently reminded us that our mission and approach were radically different from those of what they scornfully referred to as the "conventional army." Our instructors were mostly senior SF noncommissioned officers—sergeants who had spent their entire careers in Special Forces. We quickly learned that "too conventional" was one of the most devastating criticisms they could level at an officer. There were good reasons for this attitude.

The conventional army concentrates on the physical destruction of the enemy force. In its work with guerrillas, the SF usually has to focus on the political, psychological subversion needed to weaken an enemy regime. Conventional warriors measure success with body counts; the unconventional SF warriors frequently work in the ephemeral areas of hearts and minds. The conventional army's contempt for the SF approach is best exemplified by the bumper sticker that reads, "Grab 'em by the balls and their hearts and minds will follow." Conventional warriors are supported by an enormous logistical apparatus that brings beans, bullets, and bandages from the homeland; the SF and the Gs must depend on the goodwill of civilian supporters. Conventional warriors usually deal with the simple environment of traditional war where the good guys and bad guys are clearly defined; the SF operates in murkier climes.

Phase 2's university ambiance and the inherently political nature of SF work afforded many opportunities for political discussions. Much of the debate revolved around Central America. El Salvador was heating up, and some of our instructors had been among the first group of advisers sent there. They were very pessimistic about the situation and seemed to consider a Communist victory inevitable.

I thought some of the instructors had rather simplistic views on the origins of the war. They described innocent, peaceful, happy little countries suddenly pounced upon by vicious foreign Communist guerrillas. This seemed to me a right-wing mirror image of the equally simplistic leftist explanation presented to me by some of the missionaries in Guatemala. I argued that repressive right-wing regimes had provided Communist insurgents with fertile ground for the seeds of revolution. Such opinions quickly got me tagged as the class leftist. A label like that could be dangerous in Special Forces school, but our debate was very civil and fair, and I enjoyed it.

An excerpt from an article I wrote about the course provides a glimpse of the politico-military nature of the program:

> In the small white wooden building off Fort Bragg's Gruber Road, the discussion had once again turned south, towards Central America. One of my classmates, Captain Robert Avey, was delivering a report on his research topic: the war in El Salvador.
>
> While describing the supply routes used by the guerrillas, he hit one of those maddening memory lapses that sometimes plague public speakers. He had momentarily forgotten the name of the small body of water that separates El Salvador from Nicaragua. "The gulf of . . . it's the gulf of . . ."
>
> As he scratched his head and racked his brain for the word that most of us knew, a major in the back of the room filled in the gap and sent the class into a burst of self-conscious, ironic chuckling.
>
> "Tonkin! It's the Gulf of Tonkin!"

Guerrilla War in the Republic of Pineland

The third and final phase of the Q course took us back to the field. To provide a setting for a realistic exercise, a synthetic country had been established in the Uwharrie National Forest of North Carolina. The instructors gave us detailed history texts of the "Republic of Pineland" and told us that the country had been invaded by a power hostile to the United States. Our mission was to parachute into Pineland and link up with an indigenous guerrilla movement that had risen to fight the enemy invaders.

The Q course cadre had really outdone themselves in preparation for this exercise. Civilian residents of the Uwharrie area had been contracted to play certain roles. Some were hostile and would report on us. Others played the role of friendly supporters. Of course, we didn't know who was who. The role of the enemy invader was played by units of the 82nd Airborne Division accompanied by SF instructors. Their mission was to find and eliminate us. Exercise realism was enhanced when we were told that captured SF students would be tortured. We knew they wouldn't really injure us, but the thought of our instructors sticking pins in us was enough to make us sincerely interested in avoiding detection and capture.

The most ingenious component of the exercise involved the fabrication of the guerrilla force that we were to assist. A makeshift band of cooks, clerks, repairmen, and other noncombat troops had been collected from all over Fort Bragg. Some had volunteered to help the SF training effort; others were being punished by their first sergeants. Dressed in civilian clothes and issued Soviet AK-47 rifles, these "guerrillas" were formed into groups of about twenty-five and placed under the leadership of an SF sergeant (in mufti) who played the role of guerrilla unit commander.

In Phase 2 we had been taught not to expect a warm greeting from the guerrilla force—there was bound to be some distrust and skepticism from guerrillas who had been fighting for some time without our assistance. Some guerrilla leaders would see us as a threat to their authority. Many of the battle-hardened G combatants would resent the presence of foreign interlopers who had not yet been tested in battle.

The exercise was designed to teach us how to work with cantankerous guerrillas. In order to turn our mock G force into a sufficiently feisty and obstreperous group, the Gs had been sent to the field several days prior to our arrival. In addition to receiving coaching from their SF "G chief," they had been made uncomfortable by the unfamiliar field environment—they had been rained on and were cold. By the time we got there they were appropriately cranky and hard to deal with.

Our work with Fort Bragg's mock Gs provided some valuable professional lessons. One night, for example, a mysterious messenger arrived in our camp and summoned the leaders of our team to a meeting of the guerrilla force high command. We had been working with one of the low-level guerrilla units; now we were going to talk to the senior leaders of the Pineland resistance movement.

Three men with AK-47s escorted us to a pickup truck. We were blindfolded and placed face down on the bed of the truck. After a deliberately disorienting ride through the countryside, we were guided into a small building. When the blindfolds were removed, we saw before us the infamous Mike Brown, leader of the Pineland resistance. Seated on his lap was a comely young woman in tight-fitting clothes.

Mike was angry. He was unhappy with our assistance. He snarled at us and called us losers. We had lost in Vietnam, so why should he listen to us? We knew from the start that it was not going to be an easy meeting.

All through SF school I had been struggling. Most of my classmates were better land navigators, parachutists, and tacticians than I. It seemed that most were better able to cope with the forced marches and the obstacle courses. But that night in the meeting with Mike Brown, I found an area in which I could excel. The team leader was having trouble dealing with Brown, so I jumped in to assist. I took over the role of chief negotiator, and after a while the talks were back on track—it soon became apparent that we would be able to win Mike Brown over to our side.

My negotiations did, however, run into one major complication. All was going smoothly until Mike Brown's girlfriend asked if we would like some coffee. Not wishing to offend, we accepted the offer.

The three of us were seated side by side at a picnic table covered by an improvised tablecloth. Brown was seated pompously in a thronelike lounge chair to our front; his lackeys sat behind us. As the talks went on, I noticed that my partners seemed to become upset when their coffee was served. I couldn't quite figure out what was going on, but I knew something was wrong when my normally unflappable team leader asked if he could stand up. He said he had hurt his knee on the truck. This man was not one to complain about a minor injury, so I knew something was wrong.

I found out exactly what was going on when Mike Brown's girlfriend served me my coffee. As we talked of guerrilla strategy, she sat down across the table from me. Suddenly I felt her bare foot sliding up the inside of my thigh. My God! Footsie at the negotiating table! I bet Henry Kissinger never had to deal with that! Facing a no-win situation ("Hey, Mike, your girlfriend here is trying to turn me on!"), I followed my chief's lead and looked for an excuse to extricate myself from this pleasant but dangerous situation. My strategy was to ask if I could move to the wall to look at a map.

We had survived our test of diplomatic skill, and I had finally found something in SF school that I was relatively good at. Following our successful talks with Mike Brown, we were able to build rapport with the G force and get our training and advisory efforts under way. Soon we were out ambushing units of the hated invader. My group managed to avoid capture. The exercise was filled with memorable incidents that reinforced the lessons we had learned about the profoundly different nature of SF operations.

Sadly, Pineland remains in enemy hands. But we can all take comfort in the knowledge that Q course students continue to fight to free the country from the grip of the evil oppressors.

Diplomats in Uniform

I graduated from SF school in mid-1983. During the training I had been a reservist on active duty only for the duration of the program. Soon after graduating and returning to civilian life, I submitted my application for full-time active duty in the U.S. Army. I asked to go to a Special Forces unit in Latin America. Months passed as the army processed my paperwork. Finally, I received a call from Washington informing me that my application had been approved. I became part of the Reagan military buildup.

I was surprised when the caller told me that I had been scheduled to attend the Foreign Area Officer (FAO) Course at Fort Bragg. The FAO course was normally reserved for much more senior officers. When I questioned the orders, I was told abruptly by the major on the telephone: "You'll go where you're sent, Lieutenant!" Not wanting to further irritate the major (and not wanting to look a gift horse in the mouth), I packed my bags and got ready to begin a four-year tour in the U.S. Army.[1]

While I had hoped to go to a Special Forces unit, I wasn't at all disappointed that I was going to the FAO course instead. I knew that the six-month program was a graduate-level course designed to prepare officers for service as attachés or in other positions that required politico-military expertise. Once again I had found my way into a very interesting army program.

While the SF course had been filled with adventure and physical challenges, the FAO course was intellectually interesting and filled with academic challenges. Although all of my classmates outranked me, I soon found myself part of another very congenial fraternity. While SF school had sent us out on field trips to plot the destruction of piers and bridges, the FAO course had us in Washington mixing it up on Embassy Row and visiting Congress.

I was assigned to the course's Latin America seminar group. We spent the next six months in sometimes bitter arguments about U.S. policy in Central America. These arguments proved to be very useful because almost everyone in our seminar was eventually sent to the region. I think it helped us to have wrestled with all of the moral and ethical issues beforehand.

I benefited most from some of the economic instruction. I took a long, hard look at "dependency theory," a popular analysis that attributes Latin American poverty and U.S. prosperity to economic exploitation by the United States. In college and during my Central American travels I had been troubled by this theory—it places the blame for Latin poverty on the shoulders of the United States. After crunching the numbers and looking at the history of development in both regions, I concluded that the dependency theory does not hold water. The United States grew rich long before it had any significant economic interaction with Latin America, and increased trade with the United States seemed more like a cure for poverty than the cause of it. I decided that the real reasons for the underdevelopment had to lie elsewhere.

The FAO course also gave me an opportunity to take a close look at what had happened in Guatemala in 1954. In that year the United States had engineered the overthrow of the Guatemalan government. Critics on the left seemed to consider this coup the seminal event in Central America's slide into repression and violence. I wrote some of my FAO course research papers on the Guatemala coup, and some of my conclusions were very close to the analysis of the left. I wrote, for example, that the coup had "prevented the continuation of a reform process that could have prevented violent revolution," and that it had "discredited democratic reform as a viable option and discredited the United States." But I also concluded that the overthrown president (Jacobo Arbenz) was in fact a Communist, and "his continuation in power was probably not in the interest of the United States."[2]

While I was studying this coup, one of the men responsible for it, David Atlee Phillips, visited Fort Bragg. Phillips (who has passed away) wrote extensively during his retirement about what happened in Guatemala, so I think I can write about my conversations with him without violating any confidences. Due to long professional habit I find it difficult to write about his background and his employer. Readers unable to figure it out should consult a Web search engine.

I arranged to be Phillips's host, and after his lecture I took him to dinner at the Fort Bragg Officers' Club. Over dessert I asked him about the moral implications of what he had done. Alluding to the leftist critique of the coup, I asked him if he felt guilty or responsible for the thirty years of violence and repression that had followed his "successful" little project.

Phillips laughed. Obviously, he had been asked that before. He told me that, no, he did not feel responsible for the mayhem in Guatemala. He pointed out (correctly, I think) that Guatemala's problems did not begin in 1954; their roots are far deeper. He scoffed at the notion that Guatemala had been a happy little country until (as the left alleges) he and his friends came along and transformed it into a slaughterhouse. He also admonished me to remember the geopolitical context in which the 1954 coup was planned. During the planning phase the United States was dealing not with a kindly Mikhail Gorbachev in the Kremlin, but with monstrous Josef Stalin.

While my own research was focused on 1950s Guatemala, most of our seminar's debate focused on the current situation in Nicaragua; 1984 was a particularly interesting year to be discussing that country. My visit to Nicaragua had diminished some of my earlier sympathy for the Sandinista experiment, but I still had not quite made up my mind. Some of my classmates seemed to share my uncertainty. We were faced with the classic Cold War questions about Third World revolutionary movements, questions presaged by the Guatemala coup of 1954: Were these people homegrown reformers simply trying to improve conditions in their own poor little country? Or were they agents of Soviet Communism working in support of Lenin's worldwide project that had the United States as its ultimate target?

This key question was quickly and definitively resolved by the fortuitous arrival of what our group called "the little red book." One of our colleagues had just completed graduate study at the University of Miami. While he was there, a fellow student named David Nolan had published a book entitled *The Ideology of the Sandinistas and the Nicaraguan Revolution*. Our colleague liked it and obtained a number of copies for us. The little red book proved to be a devastating and scrupulously documented indictment of Sandinismo. In searing detail Nolan described the deliberate deceptions perpetrated by the Sandinistas: how they hid behind a facade of moderation while cynically building the infrastructure for draconian, totalitarian rule; how they presented themselves as unaligned nationalists when in fact they were agents of our strategic enemy. In short, Nolan showed the Sandinistas to be wolves in sheep's clothing.[3]

While Nolan's book effectively ended our debate on the nature of Sandinismo, we continued to discuss what the United States should do about the Nicaragua problem. Some of the more conventionally oriented members of the seminar were clearly salivating at the possibility of launching a massive U.S. invasion. They focused almost exclusively on the quantities of personnel and hardware that would be needed to destroy the Sandinista military forces and spoke confidently about the number of days or weeks that would be needed to complete the operation. Even though they were in a course designed to inculcate politico-military expertise, they ignored the political complications.

I did not think such an invasion would be a wise move for the United States. A bipartisan commission led by Henry Kissinger had published a report that cited the Soviet Union's desire to create conditions in Central America that would require the United States to commit large forces to the region. A U.S. invasion of Nicaragua would thus—whatever the outcome—hand our chess-playing Soviet adversaries a kind of victory. While our attention and resources were diverted in Nicaragua, the Soviets might take advantage of the situation to make a move elsewhere.

Nor was I sure that such an invasion would be successful. I didn't doubt the U.S. military's ability to blow up Nicaraguan tanks, but I had grave doubts about our ability to deal with the complexities of what would almost certainly evolve into a nasty guerrilla war. In Beirut, one bomb had driven our marines back onto their boats. How long would the American people put up with daily casualty reports from Nicaragua? Not very long, I thought.

Finally, I didn't think it was necessary to send in U.S. troops. We had other options that were less costly and less risky. My recent Special Forces training had opened my eyes to the benefits of surrogate warfare. If the United States could work successfully with indigenous forces, it might not be necessary to commit our own troops. That was the way the Soviets worked. It seemed sensible to me. I thought we should take a shot at using the contra option.

We also argued a lot about the way U.S. policy was being explained—or not explained—to the American people. We had some revealing encounters with the Washington officials involved in the public relations effort. In one instance an army colonel working for the State Department's Office of Public Diplomacy came to Fort Bragg and lectured us about his work and the war. We asked him about reports of massive human rights violations by the Guatemalan army. Members of our seminar—who had been looking quite closely at the problem—were surprised when the colonel rather glibly attributed the violations to "biased reporting by left-wing journalists." I wondered how the colonel hoped to win the support of the American people when he couldn't even gain the confidence of a group of very sympathetic U.S. Army officers.

A second incident involved a civilian official from the same office. At the conclusion of his lecture at the Special Warfare Center, I asked him a simple question: "Knowing what we know about the Sandinistas, why don't we publicly and overtly support the contras rather than providing covert support?" The visitor cleared his throat, fiddled with his papers, and finally said, "I'm afraid I don't have an answer to your question." Obviously, there were major problems with the way the U.S. government was presenting our contra policy to the public.

I was very happy to be in the FAO course, but some in the class suspected that in spite of all the strategic-level coursework and Capitol Hill schmoozing, the area studies program was not on the army's fast track to promotion. That didn't bother me, but some of the more senior officers in the class seemed to be concerned. So the scheduled lecture of a senior Fort Bragg general officer created a lot of hopeful expectation. This general was an FAO. He was one of us who had made it big. I think some of my colleagues were hoping that he would provide some career tips, or at least a bit of encouragement.

The general gave us a very interesting lecture about his FAO assignments in Moscow and Beijing. We were impressed by his mastery of Russian and Chinese (and other languages). But his comments on the army's attitude toward our work were not encouraging: "Gentlemen, I have to tell you, I became a general not because I'm a Foreign Area Officer. I became a general in spite of being a Foreign Area Officer." This statement hit the class with an almost audible thud. You could almost feel the cold pail of water extinguishing dreams of promotion; you could almost hear the rustling of applications for early retirement.

PSYOP

As my graduation from the FAO course approached, I think somebody in the army figured out that someone had made a mistake in sending a mere lieutenant to the prestigious Foreign Area Officer Course. When the personnel officers came down to hand out our postgraduation assignments, it became clear that the bureaucracy intended to have its revenge. While I would have liked duty in an embassy as an assistant attaché or security assistance officer, the major from Personnel took obvious pleasure in bluntly condemning me to what he apparently thought would be a punishment tour in a Fort Bragg psychological operations (PSYOP) battalion.

In the macho world of Fort Bragg, the operators of military loudspeakers and the producers of leaflets and radio programs are not considered the coolest guys on the block. As members of an outfit that does not fit well into the traditional military scheme of things, the PSYOP troops are the victims of the same kind of scorn the conventional army heaps on the Special Forces, but they do not have the compensation of being an elite organization. The SF is elite, misunderstood, and much maligned; PSYOP is just misunderstood and much maligned.

The conventional military's scorn for PSYOP was brought home to me by the way one senior officer described the difference between the two models of O-2 airplanes. The O-2 is a small, Cessna-like military plane. It comes in two configurations: an attack version (the A model) fitted with weapons, and a PSYOP version (the B model) that can carry loudspeakers and disperse leaflets. "You know how I remember the difference between the model numbers?" asked the officer. "A is for Attack. B is for Bullshit."

But I realized that there was no point in arguing with the major from Personnel. Besides, I saw some possibilities in PSYOP.

Before I was sent to the PSYOP battalion, I was put through a ten-week course on psychological operations. The course confirmed my suspicions that the rigid and doctrinaire army had absolutely no feel for the amorphous and imprecise art of political warfare. The course was mostly useless. I amused myself by writing a long paper on Guatemala and spent my spare time hanging out with the foreign students assigned to the course.[4]

On the day I reported for duty to the commander of my new unit, I knew that my instinct about PSYOP having some potential was correct. The battalion commander asked me two questions:

"Are you single?"

"Yes sir."

"Do you speak Spanish?"

"Yes sir."

At that point he told me to go to the arms room to get a weapon. On my first day in the battalion, while still dressed in the Class B uniform I had worn for graduation from the PSYOP course, I was preparing to draw a .45-caliber pistol and equipment for a mission in Central America. I was off to a good start and could not have been happier.

My deployment to Honduras in March 1985 marked the beginning of two and a half years of army-financed adventure in Central America. I was involved in most of the big exercises that brought thousands of U.S. troops to the region. I periodically lived in the temporary U.S. facilities at Palmerola Air Base in central Honduras. For almost nine months I was attached to Headquarters, U.S. Southern Command (SOUTHCOM) in Panama; I kept a room in the Fort Bragg BOQ, but it was more of a storage closet than living quarters—I was rarely there.

I lived a charmed life: I had travel orders that authorized me to go anywhere in Central America. I was authorized to use hotel rooms and rental cars wherever I landed. As I became more involved in SOUTHCOM projects, my travel became more and more frequent—during 1985 I changed countries twenty-seven times. I moved so often that sometimes, upon waking, I had to peer out of the hotel window and examine the skyline to remember where I was.

That much moving around, especially in underdeveloped countries, is not good for your health. In spite of heeding the admonition to not drink the water, I was frequently sick. Especially in the early days of my work in the region, my digestive system was often held together by large doses of Lomotil. My first visit to the Honduran General Staff Headquarters was a real Central America nightmare: my head was spinning (probably because I had lost so much fluid); I was still struggling with Spanish; the Honduran colonel was being difficult; the headquarters itself was hot, noisy, and confusing—there were chickens running around in the central courtyard. When I returned to Fort Bragg after that trip, I had lost so much weight that the people in my battalion headquarters did not recognize me when I showed up to turn in my weapon.

I traveled on military airplanes when I could and on commercial flights when necessary. Once, while I was snoozing next to the runway in Tegucigalpa's airport, waiting for a C-130 to take me back to Panama, the aide of SOUTHCOM's commander in chief (General Galvin) kicked my boot and asked if I wanted to fly back in style on the general's 707. Sometimes the commercial flights resulted in weird layovers. I always found it exciting when the plane put down in Managua and I saw Soviet-made helicopters on the runway. It was fun to land in an enemy capital. Other flights went through San Salvador and included a six-hour layover with (in spite of the war) optional trips to the beach or to the city's Sheraton Hotel.

Most of the U.S. military exercises in Central America were simply more realistic versions of the maneuvers army units routinely engaged in back home. A unit at Fort Bragg would pack up personnel and equipment, climb onto transport planes, and fly to Honduras to play a role in a prearranged scenario. The deployment itself—the preparing and packing and loading and unloading—

often provided the most valuable lessons. The deployments frequently came without much warning, and we were always told to be tight-lipped about destinations and departure times. Once, as I frantically packed my rucksack and duffle bag in the Fort Bragg BOQ, I noticed that my neighbor—a helicopter pilot—was doing the same thing. We both followed the rules and didn't reveal our deployment plans, but a few days later we crossed paths on a hilltop in central Honduras.

The exercises were very educational for everyone involved. Units learned a lot about preparing for sudden travel to remote and hostile areas, and the troops usually got a kick out of going to a foreign country. Officers were practicing how to take their units to war. For me, the most sobering lessons involved contemplating the enormous responsibilities that we as officers had for the health and safety of the soldiers entrusted to us. When some of my troops came close to having a serious road accident, I began to understand how bad losses in a real war would be. I was upset for a long time at the thought that I had almost lost some of them. After the completion of one of the exercises, I had to leave one of my men at the base at Palmerola to look after some equipment that was awaiting transport back to the United States. I knew that he was well cared for at Palmerola, but I felt guilty about leaving him behind and could not relax until he was safely home.

Some of the exercises were massive operations involving thousands of men, tanks, helicopters, and airplanes. The organizational and logistical challenges were enormous. When I walked through the door at the U.S. headquarters facility during exercise Solid Shield '87, I found a complex of enormous portable buildings that had been flown to Honduras from the United States. Scores of busy staff officers worked in air-conditioned comfort amidst the same collection of fax machines, typewriters, and water coolers that you would find at their headquarters back home. Outside was Honduras; inside was the United States.

The troops were aware of the contrasts and quickly developed an "us versus them" mentality. In a sarcastic variation on the stereotypical opening line for army war stories, the graffiti on a latrine wall declared: "There I was, COMPLETELY surrounded by HONDURANS!" The adversarial mindset affected even our language-skilled and culturally sensitive PSYOP soldiers: from the conventional troops they picked up the bad habit of referring to all Hondurans as "Hondos." Salvadorans were "Salvos." I was once horrified to hear a Special Forces team refer to their Central American students as "LBGs" (little brown guys). I tried my best to stamp out this kind of language and thinking in my little corner of the army: I used my dictatorial powers and imposed a push-up penalty for anyone heard using dehumanizing terms.

During one of the exercises, we took our entire battalion and all of its equipment (including large printing presses and broadcast radio stations) and set up operations on the north coast of Honduras. Other operations took me elsewhere in Honduras, usually in the company of small teams of PSYOP specialists. We shot a video in the remote Yoro Valley. We supported civic action projects in horribly poor areas near the Gulf of Fonseca. We accompanied Special Forces teams on training missions in the remote province of Olancho. On the shores of the Gulf of Fonseca I came across friends from the Special Forces course and met a crusty old SF team sergeant who, as we sat around a campfire, told me that we were all players in what he termed the "Low Intensity, High Per Diem War." He seemed worried that it might someday be over.

The young American soldiers were often stunned by the living conditions of the Hondurans. Sometimes they took matters into their own hands. During one exercise, our chaplain had placed a donations box near our mess hall tent, and troops were asked to donate portions of their field rations. The troops dropped off unopened candy bar packets, cans of franks and beans, and so on. Near the end of our deployment we put together a delegation to go to Tegucigalpa to deliver the food to an orphanage. During the visit, one of our sergeants noticed a little girl with a crippled leg. In talking to the orphanage staff the sergeant discovered that the child needed a brace, but no money was available to get one for her. I later found out that he consulted with doctors back home and, on a subsequent trip to Honduras, brought a brace for the little girl's leg.

Many of our soldiers were from the inner city, but even with their tough, underprivileged backgrounds they were still shocked by the deadly poverty they encountered in southern Honduras. They always wanted to do something to help. Previous medical civic action projects had brought army doctors to the villages, and the people assumed any American in uniform was a doctor—they came running up to us seeking medical help. Many were in horrible condition. During one very memorable visit, a young mother with bulging, desperate eyes and two very sick, malnourished babies, one under each arm, ran up to us asking us for help. Our troops were seeing things that in the States would have warranted a 911 call and the dispatch of an ambulance. But in southern Honduras there was no help to call.

Exhibiting a classically American cultural characteristic, the troops asked me what the United States was doing to fix the problem of Honduran poverty. When I told them "not much," they were angry and frustrated. Young

Americans were simply not used to such massive problems that so obstinately defied quick American solutions.

At the American Military Base in Central America

Joint Task Force Bravo (JTF-B), located on Palmerola Air Base in Honduras, provided the infrastructure to support the big military exercises. At Palmerola we had the hospital, helicopter, communications, and logistical assets needed to support the mock war effort. JTF-B became more comfortable and institutionalized over the years, but it was never considered a permanent organization. We had to be careful about referring to Palmerola as "an American base"—that would have irritated both Honduran nationalists and Americans opposed to our presence in Central America. But the portion of the Honduran facility where the thirteen hundred Americans lived was very much an American base.

I became very comfortable there. During my last stay on the base I was given two little buildings on the far side of the airfield where I led an almost bucolic existence. Stepping out of my "hooch" on a spectacular Honduran morning, I would take in the beautiful panorama of the enormous Comayagua Valley: brilliant green terrain and bright blue sky, and an almost flat valley floor sharply defined by steep mountains. As we did our morning runs around the airfield perimeter we exchanged greetings with the farmers who tilled the land on the other side of the fence. Sometimes we went bicycle riding. Everything we needed was close at hand: mess hall, barber shop, PX, gymnasium, movie theaters, swimming pools, officers' club—all the comforts of home had been miniaturized and grafted onto the Honduran landscape. While life at Fort Bragg had been much like living in a lonely American suburb, life at Palmerola was fraternal, communal. I liked it.

One of my last jobs in the army involved setting up a small PSYOP team at Palmerola. That is how I got the two buildings—and credit for inventing a new army acronym. The team that used these little buildings was intended to provide psychological operations support to the commander of U.S. forces at Palmerola. It was all very benign and innocent: we would explain to the Honduran population what U.S. forces were doing, defuse rumors, and that kind of thing. But the sinister-sounding name "PSYOPS" might have blocked approval for the project. So one afternoon in 1987 at Fort Bragg I came up with the idea of calling the team the Military Information Support Team, or MIST. Thus was born a new army program and acronym.

Soon we had our own little operation on the far side of the runway, far from base headquarters and the base bureaucracy, where the team could work without too much harassment from above. We organized a nightly "Evening at the Movies" to keep our troops entertained in their off-hours. We had brought a large amount of video equipment to use in our day-to-day work, and each night we used it to show movies that we rented through the PX.

We had also brought a large stock of archival video that we used in putting together our own television products. One piece from the archives never failed to raise goose bumps when we showed it before the "Evening at the Movies" main feature. During the 1980 campaign, the Republicans used a video with a country-and-western song made famous by singer Lee Greenwood called "I'm Proud to Be an American." It may seem corny now, but many of us sitting there in that little shack at the base of the Comayagua Valley felt lumps in our throats when we heard that song. Because of the ideological nature of our work, our troops had a good idea of what the Cold War was all about and why we were in Central America. It was a very patriotic group.

It was always interesting (and a little eerie) to watch the activities of the American military population in that Honduran valley. Older career soldiers who came to Palmerola almost inevitably commented that the place looked like a Vietnam base camp. One Friday night, a U.S. rock group was brought down to entertain the troops. As the sun set and a cooling breeze finally started to blow through the hot valley, hundreds of young Americans in jungle fatigues started to gather around the improvised stage. The rock musicians occasionally had to compete with the noise of arriving Hueys—the helicopter that had come to symbolize a war that most of the troops were too young to remember. Listening to the familiar American rock music in that profoundly foreign landscape conjured up my own (secondhand) images of Vietnam: it was reminiscent of scenes from the movie *Apocalypse Now*. "Why are all these young Americans here in this foreign place?" I asked myself.

It started out as saber rattling. While it is true that the U.S. armed services wanted exercises to improve the proficiency of our troops, and wanted to conduct these exercises in realistic overseas settings, the main purpose of the exercises was to present a warning to the Sandinistas. We wanted to remind them that we could quickly and effectively move our forces into the region. Unfortunately, as time passed and the Sandinistas became more firmly established, the tactic lost its effect. After a few years, the sound of rattling sabers seemed to fade into the background noise.

By the time I left Honduras in 1989, it seemed to me that much of the strategic logic behind the exercise program had disappeared and that the exercises were continuing through sheer bureaucratic inertia. The base had been set up, and multiyear exercise programs had been built around it, so even though the original rationale for the base was disappearing, no one seemed to be considering packing up and going home.

Early one morning in July 1988, I was en route from Tegucigalpa to Palmerola Air Base on routine embassy business (by this time I was out of the army and in the Foreign Service). When I stopped by the embassy before leaving Tegucigalpa, I found the marine guards recovering from a very busy and tense night. A group of American servicemen from Palmerola had been attacked by terrorists in the Honduran city of San Pedro Sula. The embassy's marines had been relaying messages on the attack and assisting in efforts to help the wounded. When I got to Palmerola, the officers there were coordinating the helicopter flights that would bring the wounded back to the base. I learned that our soldiers had been on a rest-and-recreation visit to the town when terrorists had sprayed their van with submachine-gun fire. Nine soldiers had been hit.

The following day I flew with the ambassador and his wife from Tegucigalpa to Palmerola to visit the injured. It was a sobering sight: nine young Americans lying in a row in the hospital ward. All of them survived. Luckily, most had been hit in the legs. One soldier who had been hit in the chest was still in great pain when we visited him. That time and every time afterward that an American GI was wounded by terrorists, I asked myself why our troops were still in Honduras. I couldn't find any good answers.

The thrust of the military exercise program was another reminder of the conventional orientation of the U.S. military. Many of the maneuvers seemed to be designed to improve our ability to defend Honduras from a conventional military invasion. On my first trip south, in March 1985, I found our troops in Honduras building tank traps near the Nicaraguan border. *Tank traps!* Apparently, officers who had spent their careers preparing for war in Europe (where attention was focused on the tank-vulnerable "Fulda gap") arrived in Honduras and started looking around for something analogous. They found it in the flatlands near Choluteca. They quickly dubbed this area the "Choluteca gap" and started preparing for the Sandinista armored onslaught. Never mind that only a collective fit of suicidal dementia would have led the Sandinistas even to consider such a loony option. Never mind that the Sandinistas probably did not have the logistical resources to mount such an operation. Never mind that subversion was clearly their preferred modus operandi (they were, in fact, already supporting armed guerrilla groups in Honduras). The motto of the U.S. Army should have been "Tanks are us!" So we built our own little Maginot Line in Choluteca, Honduras.

I often thought that the U.S. exercise program and military aid effort in Honduras was analogous to the construction of a big, deadly catapult. We built the catapult and kept it aimed at Nicaragua. We periodically practiced loading it, and we proudly drove it around for show. But our enemies were never stupid enough to give us cause to fire it. While we were brandishing our catapult, they were secretly spreading subversive termites around its base. The termites quietly ate away at the foundation, but we didn't even notice; the "security" provided by our magnificent machine blinded us to the real subversive threats that surrounded us.

Panama and the Southern Command

Because SOUTHCOM had no psychological operations assets of its own, a few people from my battalion and I had been sent there to help out with Central American projects. So while I was formally stationed at Fort Bragg, for much of this period I was actually operating out of Panama.

Like many people at SOUTHCOM, my professional attention was focused elsewhere—in my case on Honduras and to a lesser extent El Salvador. Panama itself seemed fairly unimportant. Everyone recognized that Manuel Antonio Noriega was running an autocratic "thugocracy" on the isthmus, but that seemed a small problem compared with the big game up north. El Salvador, Honduras, and Guatemala were part of the worldwide struggle against the evil empire. Americans who went up there had to worry about getting shot by Communist guerrillas. Panama, in comparison, seemed like a relatively minor crime problem.

I developed a rather unusual itinerant lifestyle during this period. I was given staff responsibility for our PSYOP program in Honduras, and soon I was making very frequent trips between Panama and Honduras. Every ninety days or so, I went back to Fort Bragg to pick up a new set of orders. I had just been promoted to captain. I had a truly remarkable amount of independence, and I was thoroughly enjoying myself. Though I had no illusions about changing the medieval ways of the American military, my group had enough small successes to keep me happy and to keep our superiors out of our hair.

But not always. . . .

When our battalion commander came down from Fort Bragg to visit us in Panama, we spent a couple of days briefing him on our projects in Central America. Throughout the briefings, something seemed to be bothering him. On the last night of his visit, over dinner at a Chinese restaurant in Panama City, he finally got it off his chest: "You need a haircut! The cut on the back of your neck is not regulation." It was true that we had grown our hair a little bit longer in an attempt to appear less obviously "American military" during our trips through the isthmus. But the colonel was still caught up in Fort Bragg's maniacal obsession with haircuts and mustache length.

This obsession was not unusual. Even in El Salvador, where U.S. advisers were being killed, many of the American commanders could not bring themselves to accept the policy of "relaxed grooming standards." A colleague in El Salvador once briefed a general officer from SOUTHCOM on operations in his sector. At the conclusion of the briefing the general's only comment was, "That mustache will be bad for your career."

After we left El Salvador, there were some leadership changes in the U.S. Military Group, and we heard that the new regime ordered military haircuts for all personnel. We were involved in an unconventional war that called for flexibility, but the haircut problem was a little reminder that we were operating under the authority of some very inflexible conventional officers.

Grooming issues aside, life in Panama in 1985 was very pleasant. I lived in the Marriott Hotel and worked in the old Canal Zone area at SOUTHCOM's Quarry Heights headquarters. When I first arrived, I was expecting to find some sort of "Pentagon South"; instead I found what looked like an old western frontier post magically transplanted into a tropical rain forest. The Quarry Heights compound was made up of dozens of old (1914-era) wooden buildings on stilts with big, wide porches. The tropical foliage completely enveloped the place. There was a little PX and a little post office; we ate lunch at the officers' club. It was like an old frontier post, but in the tropics.

The frontier fort comparison was valid for another reason: we were in many ways very isolated from Panama. Most of our work was focused elsewhere, and a "base-colony" mentality permeated the U.S. community. Panama City was just outside the gate, but SOUTHCOM television (we had our own English-language TV and radio network) regularly advertised tours of the city for the military families, many of whom would not venture off the base on their own. That was understandable. While Panama was very tame by Central American standards, it was very foreign and intimidating for many of the military dependents.

Our isolation and focus on other countries yielded a side benefit: at the working level we were not at all cozy with Panama's problematic military. In stark contrast to El Salvador and Honduras, where we worked closely with the host country officers, in Panama we lived (thankfully) in a world apart. In all my time in Panama I never so much as shook hands with one of Noriega's military officers.

While Panama itself was mostly calm in 1985, two years later, when I returned on one of my last army missions, there were indications that the people were starting to get fed up with Noriega's corrupt and dictatorial regime. There were big demonstrations. A Panamanian storekeeper with whom I had regularly debated U.S. policy (she was always complaining about U.S. meddling in Panama) grabbed my arm and said quietly, "When are you going to do it? When are you going to get rid of him?" She hadn't long to wait.

Milicrats

Late in 1985, SOUTHCOM and Fort Bragg were looking for someone to go into El Salvador to fill in for a U.S. PSYOP adviser who needed to see his family during the Christmas holidays. I was selected and ended up having a green Christmas in El Salvador. When I arrived, I was told that the Communist guerrillas had circulated leaflets announcing that they intended to send President Reagan some Christmas presents: U.S. military advisers in wooden boxes. I was struck by how different Communism seemed now that I was directly involved with it: it was suddenly a very real organization with real people and real bullets, not some vague philosophical idea; it was a physical threat to my existence, not some right-wing bogeyman.

I expected this two-week visit to be the end of my experience with El Salvador, but early the next year SOUTHCOM and the Salvadorans cooked up the idea of a PSYOP training program. The pool of potential trainers was very small, and my Christmas trip to El Salvador gave me a bit of an advantage. My battalion commander came down to Panama to discuss the project. On his last night there, while we were driving over the bridge that spans the Panama Canal, he told me that I had been picked for the El Salvador training mission. I was very pleased and immediately started making preparations.

I eventually did go on this mission, but not before overcoming some discouraging obstacles. I describe them here because they say a lot about the atmosphere in the U.S. Army during this period.

When I went back to Fort Bragg to carry out the mission planning and preparation, the army bureaucracy jumped in and tried to prevent me from going to El Salvador. Because I had been on the road so much, I had on several occasions exceeded the 180-days-per-year limit on "temporary duty" (TDY; i.e., duty away from my post of assignment, Fort Bragg). Normally, this bureaucratic obstacle was easily overcome by a short letter stating that the excessive travel was "unavoidable." But now it seemed that some of the Fort Bragg milicrats were in a huff about the amount of resources the SOUTHCOM milicrats were pulling out of their budget. They were particularly displeased that SOUTHCOM was treading on their bureaucratic turf by specifying which Fort Bragg officers were needed for the El Salvador missions. So, taking advantage of an opportunity to tweak SOUTHCOM's nose, the Fort Bragg milicrats insisted on a strict interpretation of the TDY travel regulations. And that meant that I would not go to El Salvador.

My boss had decided that my language skills, experience in El Salvador, and availability made me the only sensible choice for the mission. The military bureaucracy, on the other hand, thought of officers as interchangeable parts in their vast green machine; any officer could do the job. This silly argument came to a head when my exasperated battalion commander sent me to see the staff officer in Special Operations Command Headquarters who was responsible for this nonsense. In the company of our battalion operations officer and the officer who was slated to go to El Salvador with me, I confronted the military bureaucracy.

Lieutenant Colonel B began the conversation with a long harangue against the enemy (SOUTHCOM). This El Salvador thing was their problem, their war; they couldn't be allowed to rob Fort Bragg of its officers at will! We had training obligations to meet! The colonel was cooking along at a slow boil when it came time for us to present our case. We mentioned that I had already been in El Salvador, knew the players, and spoke the language. These comments seemed to enrage the colonel.

"Goddamn it, don't give me any of that touchy-feely bullshit! Nobody in this army is indispensable! Any good army officer could do this mission!"

This might seem like an unimportant little bureaucratic spat, but Lieutenant Colonel B's angry comments in fact reflected beliefs that had deep roots in the U.S. Army, roots that went back to the early days of the counterinsurgency in Vietnam.

In a May 1985 article in the journal *Military Review*, Col. John Waghelstein, a Special Forces officer who commanded Military Group El Salvador's army element, notes that senior army officers resisted President Kennedy's efforts to get the army to adapt to the special requirements of counterinsurgency. Gen. George Decker (army chief of staff, 1960–62) had rejected the notion that special skills were required and had said that "any good soldier can handle guerrillas." Gen. Earle Wheeler (army chief of staff, 1962–64) had said, "The essence of the problem in Vietnam is military." And Gen. Maxwell Taylor (chairman of the Joint Chiefs of Staff, 1962–64) had commented that counter-insurgency "is just a form of small war, a guerrilla operation in which we have a long record against the Indians. Any well-trained organization can shift the tempo to that which might be needed in this kind of situation."[5]

Lieutenant Colonel B continued his diatribe: "In Southeast Asia I was parachuted in to serve as an adviser. I didn't speak the language; I didn't know the 'players.' But I accomplished the mission."

I diplomatically suppressed the urge to remind the colonel that we had lost that war. Instead I pressed our request for a waiver of the suddenly enforced 180-day rule.

Now really pissed off, Lieutenant Colonel B pounded his fist on his desk and yelled, "Goddamn it, Captain, I'm a bureaucrat! The rules say 180 days. You ain't goin' to El Salvador."

I was stunned. A lieutenant colonel in the U.S. Army Special Operations Command had boldly proclaimed himself to be a bureaucrat. My surprise must have showed, because the colonel asked me why I was "giving him that look."

"Sir, I'm aghast to hear you say that!"

At this point the battalion operations officer escorted me out of the office before the colonelcrat reached critical mass. After a Herculean effort by my commander, the waiver was granted and I went to El Salvador. I was briefly famous in my battalion for the "I'm aghast" remark.

Almost a year later, after the successful completion of the El Salvador mission, I was passing through the receiving line at an official military social function. One of the senior officers (another colonelcrat who had never said anything to me about what we had accomplished in El Salvador) fixed me with a look of contempt and said, "Ah, Captain Meara. Colonel B's friend." I got the message. My bureaucratic transgression had not been forgotten. Cold War and Reagan doctrine notwithstanding, Fort Bragg and the U.S. Army were still stultifyingly bureaucratic during the 1980s.

CHAPTER 4
EL SALVADOR

The skillful leader subdues the enemy's troops without any fighting;
he captures their cities without laying siege to them; he overthrows
their kingdom without lengthy operations in the field. With his forces
intact he disputes the mastery of the empire, and thus, without
losing a man, his triumph is complete.

—*The Art of War* by Sun Tzu

MY PARTNER AND I WERE MOVING THROUGH the randomized rituals of going to work in El Salvador. Following breakfast (at a nonroutine hour in a nonroutine restaurant) we got into our recently exchanged, nondescript rental car and drove to work on a randomly selected route. As members of the U.S. Military Group (MILGRP), the branch of our embassy responsible for providing military training and assistance to the Salvadoran armed forces, we had automatic reservations on the assassination list of the Faribundo Martí National Liberation Front—the FMLN. We were following the recommendations of the security experts: civilian clothes, no routines, no regular routes, stay alert, travel in pairs. It had taken only a short time for us to grow accustomed to our new lifestyle; we had even started to joke about it. As we put on our sunglasses and checked the handguns that we were required to carry, we would sometimes joke about the movielike quality of our life in the tropics.

El Salvador was a place that called for teamwork. Capt. Hugh McPherson and I took care of each other and looked for opportunities to bolster each other's morale. I knew that Hugh missed his family, so I was on the lookout for opportunities to cheer him up. On this particular morning I surprised him by popping in a tape containing the theme music from the then-popular television series *Miami Vice* (which dealt with the adventures of two Miami Police Department detectives engaged in tropical derring-do). Hugh chuckled as we sped out of the parking lot on yet another journey to adventure—this time accompanied by the theme song from *Miami Vice*. In El Salvador, you had to have a sense of humor.

In May 1986, after months of preparation at Fort Bragg, I had finally been sent to El Salvador. The mission of our two-man team was to train members of the Salvadoran armed forces (the ESAF) in the art and science of psychological operations, a sinister-sounding but benign form of conflict that plays a key role in guerrilla warfare. Our job was to teach the Salvadorans the mass communication and public relations techniques that would help them win the battle for the hearts and minds of the Salvadoran people.

Back at Fort Bragg, Hugh and I had prepared for the course with true missionary zeal. We saw ourselves as warriors fighting the evil empire, and we were determined to do our best to make a useful contribution to the Cold War effort. We immersed ourselves in study of Cold War conflict in the Third World. We read books by Gen. Edward Geary Lansdale (USAF) about his counterinsurgency experiences in Asia, and Jean François Revel's *How Democracies Perish*. We read Bernard Fall's Vietnam classic, *Street without Joy*, and Robert Taber's guerrilla warfare primer, *War of the Flea*.

Our ideological zeal may seem silly now, but at that time the Cold War was still on, the Berlin Wall was still up, and the Soviet Union still appeared to be a clear and present danger. Radio Moscow broadcast a dehumanized, machinelike voice that droned out anti-American invective with an Orwellian tone. Cold War reality was even seeping into popular culture. Among the best-selling books in 1986 was Tom Clancy's *The Hunt for Red October*, a tale of Cold War submarine conflict. Actor Tom Cruise dueled with MiGs in the movie *Top Gun*. The British pop artist Elton John was singing a sad song called "Nikita" about someone trapped on the wrong side of the Iron Curtain. The Cold War was under way, and the evil empire was palpably and audibly evil. We were enthusiastic about making a contribution to the struggle against Communism. In the "cult of national security," we were definitely in the priesthood.

As I prepared for the deployment, I frequently felt my father and my grandfather and all of my uncles looking over my shoulder. They had all gone overseas in the service of Uncle Sam—my father had been seriously wounded while defending his ship (the USS *Ross*) during the battle of Leyte Gulf. I felt like I was following in their footsteps, and I felt a strong obligation to do my best.

We arrived during a relative lull in the fighting: 1986 was not a particularly bloody year in the chronology of Salvadoran mayhem. The years 1981–83 had been far worse, and 1988–89 would prove to be even more violent. It was just before the onset of the Iran-contra scandal—just before the El Salvador–based supply plane carrying arms to the Nicaraguan contras was shot down and the whole covert affair unraveled.

If I had arrived in El Salvador under other circumstances or in a different decade, I probably would not have been so impressed by the place, but I arrived there on a mission, and my memories will always be conditioned by that mission. Task and location combined to make El Salvador very exciting.

It was also very beautiful. During the rainy season the countryside was lush and green; conical volcanoes punctuated the landscape. Sometimes nature itself seemed to join in the violence. On one day that began with a not-too-distant FMLN bomb blast, the temperature rose all through the morning. By lunchtime the city was baking under the hot sun. Then dark clouds blew in and wild thunderstorms accompanied by hail (unusual in Central America) shook the city. For nature's grand finale, the afternoon ended with a 6.4 earthquake that sounded like a freight train and knocked McPherson and me to the ground. The message seemed clear: Beware! You are in a very wild place!

Our excitement is not hard to explain. Take two young officers who are intensely interested in Latin America and committed to the battle against Communism. Free them from the stifling army bureaucracy of Fort Bragg and send them to a small tropical country at war. Give them a mission that could have a real impact on the war. Add some danger. Throw in some pretty women (an important factor for the bachelor on the team), fairly decent hotels, and concealed handguns. It's a recipe for excitement. I was twenty-seven years old and thought this was all very cool.

We were prepared for the worst El Salvador and our mission could throw at us. Before we left Fort Bragg we went through a short training course for advisers destined for dangerous climes. We learned to operate a variety of pistols and exotic submachine guns, and we were schooled in the appropriate responses to assassination attempts. ("Gentlemen, always be sure to 'double-tap': shoot the bastard at least twice.") It was a no-nonsense preparation: we were "goin' to war in El Salvador."

I didn't tell my parents where I was going (whenever I called home I let them think I was calling from Panama). Hugh and I drew up our wills and took out expensive life insurance policies that did not contain any war/terrorism/assassination provisos. The Fort Bragg dentists took panoramic X-rays of our teeth (to aid in possible future efforts to identify remains). It was great fun—we were going off to do exciting things in a dangerous place.

And a dangerous place it was. In June 1985, four American marines assigned to the U.S. embassy had been gunned down in the capital. When I first arrived in El Salvador six months later, the embassy's mandatory security briefing for newly assigned personnel included a lot of information on that attack. Naturally, it was quite disturbing. Some of the other new arrivals apparently had not been following world news and hadn't realized what they were getting into. We heard that a group of contractors brought down to do some work on the embassy's plumbing returned to their hotel after the briefing, packed up their stuff, and headed for the airport, never to return.

We lived in the hotels of San Salvador, dividing our time among three of them. My favorite was the Sheraton. Built in the exclusive Escalon neighborhood on the slopes of the volcano that looms above San Salvador, it had a pleasant staff and a nice restaurant. From the top floor of the Sheraton I could see the Guazapa volcano—frequently home to large FMLN units. The rumble of A-37 warplanes emptying their bomb racks on Guazapa frequently provided background noise for early-morning tennis matches. The wealthy residents of Escalon didn't let the noise (or the war) interrupt their games.

Security rules severely restricted our travel around town, but the Sheraton wasn't a bad place in which to be restricted. It was a cage, but a gilded cage. Interesting people came to the Sheraton, and interesting things happened there. In 1981, two American labor advisers were assassinated in one of the restaurants by right-wing thugs. Three years after we left, the Sheraton became the focus of international attention when FMLN guerrillas attacked the hotel and briefly cornered a number of foreign guests—including the secretary general of the Organization of American States and a U.S. Army Special Forces team.

Our most dramatic event in the Sheraton involved the arrival of a platoon of heavily armed soldiers who surrounded the open-air restaurant while my partner and I were dining. We assumed that they were security for some visiting head of state and stupidly continued our dinner. Later we learned that an FMLN assassination squad en route to the hotel had been fortuitously intercepted by a Salvadoran army patrol. Our dinner could easily have been much more eventful.

For a variety of reasons, El Salvador was a great place to be a bachelor (but then again, just about anyplace in the world would have been an improvement over Fort Bragg, North Carolina). The women were very pretty. History books say that during World War II, the London Blitz seemed to serve as a catalyst for amorous activity. I think a similar effect was at work in San Salvador during the war years. True to form, however, the U.S. Army was right there doing its best to make the troops miserable. After a U.S. adviser was assassinated while waiting to meet his Salvadoran girlfriend, the army decided to take us out of harm's way by forbidding any form of romantic contact with Salvadoran women. The words from MILGRP's voluminous rulebook are burned into my memory: "Relationships of a romantic or sexual nature are specifically prohibited." Welcome to El Salvador! Have a real good time! We joked that it was a good thing the adviser hadn't been killed while dining—we might have starved.

Jokes aside, I found MILGRP's rules a sad indictment of a very bureaucratic American military. Many of them seemed designed to provide our leaders with bureaucratic cover in the event of our untimely, FMLN-sponsored demise. Some were difficult to comply with on a day-to-day basis. We were supposed to have our radios on at all times, for instance, but the radio chatter made it hard to sleep. The rules forbade us to travel alone, but occasionally I had to journey outside the hotel on short notice without being able to arrange for a bodyguard. These kinds of regulations had a negative effect on morale.

I found the "no romance" rule particularly distressing. I was at a point in my life when I was starting to hope to meet a woman to settle down with,[1] but the army seemed to be trying to rule out that possibility. I didn't like being treated like an untrustworthy child. This rule was also an excellent example of the pervasive "us-versus-them" mentality of the U.S. military—all Salvadoran women were apparently in the "them" category.

The MILGRP rules engendered an atmosphere of suspicion and distrust among the Americans in El Salvador. My partner and I kept to ourselves and didn't socialize with any other members of MILGRP—there was always the possibility that an acquaintance would discover some violation of the rules and talk about it in the embassy. I think others felt the same way. During my first visit in 1985, I spent Christmas alone in a dingy San Salvador hotel—there wasn't a lot of camaraderie. (But there was some comic relief: I had gone to bed early hoping to sleep through my lonely Christmas Eve but was then awakened by the sound of machine-gun fire. Suspecting an FMLN attack, I rolled out of bed, grabbed my pistol, and low-crawled to the window. Peering out and then looking at my watch, I realized that the Salvadorans were just having some fun, celebrating the holiday with their traditional yuletide volleys of gunfire. The tracers added a festive touch. Ho! Ho! Ho!)

As I approached the end of my mission, my anxiety level started to rise. I wasn't worried about getting killed by the FMLN—I was worried about getting caught by MILGRP in some violation of their rules: caught traveling without my Salvadoran bodyguard, caught not having my radio on. . . . And of course there was that very problematic celibacy rule. Rumor had it that a senior MILGRP officer was in the habit of sending his Salvadoran driver out to the bars and discos to see if any of us were out violating the rules against romance. In El Salvador, we were not a band of brothers.

Faced with FMLN guns and MILGRP rules, paranoia was called for—and paranoia prevailed. We really trusted no one, not even the people we were working with. An innocent "What are you doing this weekend?" during the course of ordinary conversation always brought up the fear of an ambush. We always lied about our plans. This kind of lying became somewhat habitual in the paranoid atmosphere of El Salvador. There was a story going around about one particularly uptight adviser who had ordered his Salvadoran bodyguard to "ride shotgun" in the backseat of the car during a date. He told the guy to keep his gun at the ready and to keep an eye on the girl: sweet romance in the tropical Cold War.

Army bureaucratic puritanism and guerrilla death threats notwithstanding, Hugh and I settled into a fairly pleasant "not routine" routine. Our duties and our adviser status kept us far from the gruesome realities of combat. We became familiar with the hotels that were our gilded cages and learned the menus of the few restaurants we were able to use. If, because of my time in El Salvador, I someday fall victim to delayed traumatic stress syndrome, I think the flashbacks will probably be triggered by good restaurants with tropical motifs. We were peripheral participants in the "Low Intensity, High Per Diem War." And we liked it.

Counterparts

For our work, my partner and I set up shop in an unused classroom of the "Capitán General Gerardo Barrios" Military Academy—the Salvadoran equivalent of West Point. Acquiring the classroom proved to be quite a chore.

In spite of more than six months of preparation, including numerous conferences with the Salvadoran armed forces, we arrived to find that no classroom space had been reserved for us. The Salvadoran officer in charge of our operation—I'll call him Colonel Robles—seemed completely baffled by our obvious disappointment. He had clearly failed to come across with the only thing we had asked him for—a classroom. We were polite and courteous in reminding him that a classroom was an essential ingredient for a successful course. He just sat there and smiled and said that there was nothing to be done. At one point he suggested that we rent a large room in the Hotel Presidente and conduct the course there. When we raised the obvious security concerns involved in doing that, he came up with a ridiculous scheme in which we would disguise ourselves and our students as participants in a Central American florists' convention. We eventually cajoled him into releasing the required classroom, but the incident provided an early reminder that we were in a very different place, dealing with institutions and people profoundly different from those we were accustomed to.

The Salvadoran military, and Salvadoran society as a whole, are not "just like ours." Most Americans naively assume that foreign countries really are—deep down—just like the United States. "Sure they speak different languages, but people are people, right?" Geographic proximity and superficial similarities reinforce this belief among Americans traveling in Latin America. Foreign visitors also often fail to realize that they are not just dealing with differences of scale. While the institutions of a foreign country may bear some superficial similarity to U.S. institutions, their roles, inner workings, and interactions with other national institutions are profoundly different from what Americans are used to. Dealing with day-to-day problems in the foreign culture is the only way to really come to understand the depth of the differences.

The institution that I dealt with in El Salvador was the armed forces, specifically the Combined General Staff Headquarters known as the Estado Mayor. The way the Estado Mayor was introduced to visiting Americans illustrates the phenomenon I am trying to describe: it was almost invariably presented as "the Salvadoran Pentagon." It took me awhile to understand how completely inappropriate this description was. I watched with amazement, for example, as the chief of the Combined General Staff—the "equivalent" of our chairman of the Joint Chiefs of Staff—was asked in a staff meeting to decide on the placement of a new photocopier. I was even more amazed when he agreed to make the decision (saying that he would need some time to study and consult).

In El Salvador we found a familiar military organization: a central headquarters with subordinate brigades. We were, however, frustrated and confused by inexplicable inefficiencies. One example: We found a few pieces of equipment lying unused at the headquarters of one of the subordinate brigades. Thinking that it could be put to good use in the General Staff Headquarters, we suggested to Robles that he—as a principal staff officer in the Estado Mayor—order the gear transferred. Robles stalled and hedged until finally, in a burst of emotion, he accused us of trying to engineer his removal from office. "Don't you know that the brigade commanders could have me fired?" he thundered. No, we had not known. Back home things didn't work that way, but in El Salvador, the brigade commanders were powerful warlords who selectively obeyed Estado Mayor orders at their own discretion. The institutions and organizational structures were outwardly similar, but the ways of doing things and interrelating were very different.

Even our strategic concerns revealed deep differences in perspective between us and the Salvadorans. We were exclusively focused on the Communist threat. This was the main focus of Salvadoran concern as well, but they were also worried about another enemy: Honduras. The two countries had fought a war in 1969. Many of the senior officers we worked with had been involved in that conflict, and there were still hard feelings. Robles often asked me about the Honduran officers I had worked with. Regardless of the name I gave him, his response would be along these lines: "Ah! A known homosexual! I fired at him with my pistol as he ran from the battlefield crying for his mother!" Robles was proud of the Salvadoran army's performance in the war, and he once told me that Tegucigalpa, Honduras, was the best city in the world for a Salvadoran to serve as a diplomat, "Because it is the one city in the world in which we Salvadorans can hold our heads high!"

Our failure to understand the concerns of our allies had caused problems early in the Central American conflict when the U.S. Army had tried to use Honduran military bases to train Salvadoran troops. The Hondurans were not at all pleased. I believe our PSYOP training course carried out the only operation that trained Honduran soldiers in El Salvador. With the somewhat grudging acquiescence of the Salvadorans, we brought two Honduran officers to San Salvador to go through our course. There was obviously some tension, but the Hondurans made it through the course without any real trouble. This latent Salvadoran-Honduran animosity was another reminder that the world often looks very different to people from different countries and different cultures.

Not wanting to seem like know-it-all gringos, we had suggested that our course be presented by a combined U.S.- Salvadoran team. The two Americans would concentrate on the theoretical, doctrinal aspects of the coursework, and the two Salvadoran officers would present the classes directly related to the situation in their country. This allowed us to divide up the coursework among four teachers while avoiding the preposterous situation of U.S. officers lecturing Salvadorans about the situation in their own country.

Our students were a mixture of ESAF civilian employees and military officers. The civilians, many of whom were women, were there because the armed forces wanted to keep able-bodied military men in combat leadership positions. Most of the military officers taking the course were disabled war veterans who were no longer capable of holding combat jobs.

The Estado Mayor assigned two capable young officers to serve as members of the instructional team. Both had received training in psychological operations in U.S. military training schools. Napoleon was a thirty-year-old captain of artillery whose military name belied a gentle and compassionate character. He was married, had one small child, and had been in the army for more than ten years. He was sick of the war, but he liked the army. Ivan was a twenty-five-year-old lieutenant of infantry who had gone directly into combat after graduating from the military academy. Wounded several times, Ivan was an acerbic character who obviously had been hardened and embittered by his combat experiences.

We worked with Napoleon and Ivan every day for four months, sharing the burdens of presenting a course that we all cared about. We socialized with them and got to know their friends and families. From them and from our students we learned more about the Salvadoran psyche and the Salvadoran military culture. As Americans grapple with the seemingly irrational actions of foreigners, it's common to hear exasperated cries that "they don't think like us." In our little classroom in El Salvador I found this to be quite true.

Hugh and I wanted to make the course interesting and enjoyable, so we built a lot of student participation into each lesson plan. Instinctively, we designed our lectures to use the Socratic method, filling each hour of instruction with thought-provoking questions. Throughout our years in school we had learned to think deductively, to question and to critique, to be skeptical and to test the validity of our professors' statements. The memorization of facts, dates, and names had been secondary.

Our Salvadoran students had not been educated that way. Most were graduates of either the military academy or one of the civilian universities of San Salvador. Many had obtained their *licenciatura*, a university degree (roughly equivalent to a BA) that entitles the holder to lifetime use of the honorific *Licenciado*. We naively looked at the superficial similarities (we were all college graduates) and failed to recognize the real differences that were just below the surface.

One afternoon early in the course I was presenting a class on the theory and practice of Marxist Leninism. Moving from the general to the particular (as all my teachers had done with me), I was trying to lead the class to the central point of the lecture: that Communist movements have exploited poverty and repression in underdeveloped countries. With prepackaged slides produced in the photo labs of Fort Bragg, I gave numerous examples of Communists working among poverty-stricken people in the countries of Asia, Africa, and Latin America. Finally I arrived at the Big Socratic Question. Flashing a slide with the question written on it (in big letters), I asked the class, "In El Salvador, which socioeconomic groups do you think the Communists would choose to work with?" There was a long pause while forty-five students feverishly copied the slide's text into their notebooks (as they did with every slide, instructors' pleas notwithstanding). The pause lengthened. I repeated the question. Blank stares. Finally, one student (with obvious frustration) complained that it was unfair of me to ask this question because I had not yet given them the information on El Salvador. Frantically searching through their copious notes, his classmates nodded in agreement. Similar scenes were repeated each time Hugh or I tried to employ Socratic questioning. Of course, the Salvadoran instructors never thought to use it.

Our students were neither stupid nor afraid of appearing to be leftist sympathizers. It was simply a matter of classroom culture. Salvadoran education (like schooling in much of the Hispanic world) is based on rote memorization. We had been taught to think deductively: Spot is a dog. Dogs like meat. So, what does Spot like? These lessons had been reinforced by many of our childhood games. In contrast, our Salvadoran students had simply been force-fed information. They had not been encouraged to question or to analyze. In this respect, at least in this classroom situation, you could safely say, "They don't think like we do." This kind of difference had profound implications for U.S.-Salvadoran interactions and affected our ability to understand each other.

Remembering that Spain was occupied (and deeply influenced) by the Moors for more than seven hundred years, I wondered if the patterns Hugh and I observed were distant results of this Islamic occupation. I'm no expert, but I understand the thinking to go like this: All knowledge comes from

Allah, and all men (including teachers) are placed in their jobs by Allah. Teachers are the conduits of revealed truth. Students should soak up information unquestioningly. There is no need to question the teachers or learn to think critically or deductively. Years later, while serving in Spain, I came across university students who had spent years cramming their heads full of facts. I also met a visiting American professor who lamented her Spanish students' relative inability to analyze new situations. (Of course, there are two sides to this cultural coin: I often heard Spaniards say that our schools are "too easy" and that our students graduate without having learned a lot of very important facts.)

Coming up with the final grades and determining who was going to graduate brought us into conflict with yet another cultural phenomenon—the Latin American desire to avoid confrontation and an aversion to the fixing of responsibility. In setting up the ground rules for our course, we and the Salvadorans had agreed to hold the students to some firm academic standards. We wanted the graduation certificate to mean something, and we wanted fear of failure to serve as an incentive for the students to study and pay attention. All the rules were clearly explained on the first day of the course.

Everything went fine until we actually had to enforce the rules. A number of the students just were not performing up to the course's standards. We gave them extra help and counseling. We warned them that they would not graduate if they did not achieve a passing average. They didn't seem to believe us, however, until we moved to throw them out of the course.

In keeping with a prior agreement with Robles, we routed the dismissal action through his office. He was horrified at the thought of dismissing even those students who had failed miserably. He refused to approve our action until he had "referred it to higher authorities." That meant that he was going to ask the chief of the Estado Mayor if it was all right for us to dismiss a few students from our little course. When I say "us," I refer to myself and my American partner; the Salvadoran instructors refused to be involved in the cold-blooded business of telling students that they had failed. We later learned that the chief of the Estado Mayor approved our action only after taking the matter up with the staff. He didn't want to decide on his own.

The Spanish language reflects this cultural aversion to fixing responsibility. In English, when we drop something we automatically say, "I dropped the plate." If somebody else dropped it, we do not hesitate to fix responsibility by saying, "He dropped the plate." Not so in Spanish, which uses a more passive construction that treats the event as "fortuitous": "¡Se me cayó!"

Responsibility is not automatically specified. The English language is a much blunter instrument than the beautiful and courtly language of Castile.

This general Latin aversion to the fixing of responsibility and the desire to avoid personal confrontation may have been reinforced in El Salvador by the violent nature of the society. We were told that San Salvador was the most courteous city on earth "because everyone is packing" (a gun, that is). Indeed, for a long time, El Salvador was a lawless place where disputes were frequently settled by gunfire. Clearly, such an environment would tend to encourage the avoidance of confrontation. I don't mean to imply that the Salvadorans are in any way inferior. Culture is not genetically determined. It is learned behavior, attitudes and beliefs that are socially transmitted from generation to genera-tion—in other words, software, not hardware.

Cultural differences have profound effects on how different groups view even very simple things. During the FAO course, for example, an American gen-eral told us about a train trip across China that he had made with his American wife. She had been shocked by the way fellow passengers cleared their nos-trils: they would simply hold one of them closed and let fly with the contents of the other. She found this disgusting and commented on it frequently. Late in the journey, while the general practiced his Mandarin with a fellow passenger, she blew her nose American-style, then daintily put the handkerchief back into her pocket. Watching this, the general's Chinese interlocutor was appalled: "She carries that around in her pocket? That's disgusting!"

I don't know if we can ever expect the rank and file of American military forces to develop high levels of cultural sensitivity. It is not something that can be inculcated with a few classes or lectures. Cultural sensitivity and aware-ness are difficult to develop even among the more educated commissioned officers (and sometimes even among Foreign Service officers). Our military has long recognized that American soldiers just do not mix well with foreign cultures. That is why they live on isolated bases like the ones I described in Panama and Honduras. That is why that rock concert at Palmerola Air Base made me uneasy. And that is one of the reasons why I thought it best to avoid the use of large U.S. military units in Central America.

In time we encountered many other cultural differences that made El Salvador a profoundly foreign place. The Salvadoran army had a completely different set of institutional value priorities. Loyalty to the officer corps super-seded almost every other loyalty. This created some tricky situations for us and opened up a Pandora's Box of intrigue. For example, we once accepted an invitation to dinner at the home of a Salvadoran officer. When we informed our superior in MILGRP, he grimaced. He told us that the officer who had invited us had been living under a very dark cloud of suspicion; some even believed him to be an FMLN collaborator. Furthermore, the officer's house was on the outskirts of the city. Paranoia kicked in, and we started worrying about the possibility of an ambush on the way to dinner. We were thus confronted with an etiquette situation never anticipated by Emily Post: What do you do when you suspect that your host may be setting you up for an ambush? We weren't sure that he was an enemy agent, and we didn't want to offend him. At the last minute we came up with a solution that was both socially graceful and foiled any possible assassination plot. Citing some vague "security concerns" (indeed!) we said that we didn't want to drive at night and suggested that he and his wife join us for dinner at our hotel.

On another occasion we noticed that one of our students was being ostracized by his colleagues. We didn't pay much attention to this until the student qualified for an honors certificate in the course. His fellow officers quietly protested. The honor student shouldn't get the award, they explained, because several years earlier the man had saved his own skin by turning over his company to the FMLN.

In both cases the officers involved were shunned and ostracized, but they were nevertheless tolerated and allowed to stay in the service. Traitors or cowards, they were first and foremost "members of the club," members of the Salvadoran officer corps. Such tolerance would have been inconceivable in the U.S. Army, where officers were routinely fired if their wives wrote bad checks at the PX. This tolerance opened the door to a paranoid atmosphere of distrust, suspicion, and intrigue that permeated the ESAF. It also made enforcement of U.S. human rights policies much more difficult.

New examples of problematic cultural differences came up almost every day. While American officers were encouraged to always do our best to interpret our commander's intent and to use initiative when executing our orders, the Salvadorans had been trained to exhibit blind, unquestioning obedience. One day a lieutenant brought a group of soldiers to move all the furniture because a conference had been scheduled to take place in our classroom (we had agreed to move for one day to a smaller adjoining room). Before the work started, I found out that the conference had been canceled. Hoping to save the troops from unnecessary labor, I told the lieutenant that the furniture movement would not be necessary. He replied that cancellation or no cancellation he had his orders and was going to move the furniture. I watched as the troops moved every bit of it into the next room—and the next morning moved it all right back where it came from.

Sometimes the cultural misunderstandings were humorous. Our classroom was usually quite warm, and my partner and I sweated quite a bit while lecturing. We also ran for exercise every day on the small enclosed track of the academy. To prevent dehydration, I constantly drank from my canteen. Every morning, in an attempt to avoid gastrointestinal illness, I walked across the grounds of the academy to fill my canteen at the water cooler in the cadets' snack bar. I was comforted by the labels that proclaimed "Agua Potable—Agua Cristal" (drinking water—crystal water), and by the fact that the water appeared to be replaced almost daily.

Every day as I walked to get my water, I passed through the snack bar's kitchen, which was run by a very old Salvadoran lady. Every day, for several months, we exchanged pleasantries as she let me use her water cooler. One day she stopped me and said, "Can I ask you a question? Why don't you just fill your canteen from the spigot over there next to your classroom?"

I tried to be diplomatic and culturally sensitive as I explained that as a foreigner, I was not yet completely accustomed to the local water, and was better off using bottled water.

The old woman looked completely puzzled as she said, "Well, that doesn't make much sense to me, because every morning before you come in here I fill this water cooler up from that same spigot!"

There were also some funny (but painful!) language lessons. One afternoon while U.S. Maj. Pedro Arbona and I were waiting to see Colonel Robles, we passed the time by chatting with the secretaries. One of them was kind enough to compliment my Spanish, but then she went on to say that she didn't think I would be able to cope with El Salvador's complicated slang.

I had been in the country only a few weeks at that point, but I had been trying hard to learn the slang. I guess I saw this as an opportunity to show off in front of both the secretaries and Major Arbona (he was my boss back at Fort Bragg), so I decided to put my Salvadoran slang to use. Just as Robles opened the door to greet us, I said jokingly in Spanish, "Come on, Major Arbona, we have work to do. We've been standing here *haciendo paja* for too long."

When every jaw in the room dropped simultaneously, I knew that I had said something wrong. We got through our meeting with Robles, but on our way out the secretaries seemed to try to avoid eye contact, burying their faces in their typewriters.

Back in our office, Arbona (a native speaker of Spanish) looked at me with disbelief and asked, "Do you know what you said up there?" I told him that I had recently learned that in Salvadoran slang *hablando paja* means "talking without purpose" ("talking rubbish"). "Yeah," said Arbona, "but that's not what you said. You said '*haciendo paja*,' which refers to an entirely different, uh . . . activity."

I was horrified to learn that I had just told the colonel's very prim and proper secretaries not that we had been wasting time talking nonsense, but instead that we had been wasting time . . . masturbating. There are many bumps and potholes on the road to foreign language fluency.

Gringos

During our mission in El Salvador, I carried a small American flag in my briefcase. I wanted a reminder of why Hugh and I were there. And I wanted to remind the Salvadorans of the same thing.

"Why do you carry that little flag?" they would ask.

"To remind myself of why I am here and who I am working for," I would answer.

We never tried to tell our students that we were in their country because of our love for El Salvador or our sympathy for their cause. We did like El Salvador, and we did sympathize with their cause, but that was not why we were there. We were in El Salvador because our superiors had decided that it was in the national interest of the United States to have us there doing what we were doing. Being straightforward about this helped keep things in perspective both for us and for our Salvadoran colleagues. Later on, when I was working with another, more politically controversial army (of Nicaraguans), I had less success maintaining this kind of detachment.

I was proud to be part of our advisory effort in El Salvador. I felt that I was part of a small, select group that was doing important work for the United States. I was one of fifty-five American advisers helping the Salvadorans take on world Communism. It was heady stuff.

Before arriving in El Salvador, I had been concerned about what I might learn about U.S. human rights policy there; I worried that I might find myself working in an organization complicit in human rights abuses. But soon after I arrived, my mind was put at ease. In addition to proscribing amorous contact with the Salvadoran population, MILGRP's policy book established strict guidelines for U.S. advisers who witnessed or became aware of ESAF human rights violations. If we came upon a human rights violation in progress—torture of prisoners, abuse of noncombatants, and so on—we were to immediately try to use our influence to stop the violation. If unable to stop it, we were to disassociate ourselves from the activity. In either case we were to immediately report the incident to the commander of MILGRP.

I was proud and relieved to find that human rights were a very real concern of the U.S. Military Group. We were not paying lip service to the subject. We were not turning a blind eye to Salvadoran abuses. And we did not tell the Salvadorans that this was something we had merely been ordered to express concern about; we always made it clear that we were personally committed to the U.S. human rights policy.

We were serious about the human rights policy, and this seriousness even affected the way we reacted to Salvadoran humor: At a drunken pool party at which Hugh and I were the only gringos (and the only sober guests), a Salvadoran lieutenant colonel told a joke about a mummy that had been found in Egypt. It seems that the Egyptians had been embarrassed by their inability to determine the mummy's age. Secretly, they had flown the remains to England for examination by British scientists. The Brits had been similarly baffled and embarrassed, and they in turn secretly passed the body to the Yanks. President Reagan boasted that American science would solve the mystery. But after three days he was told that even our best scientists had been unable to determine the mummy's age.

At the moment the president was informed, he was meeting with the Salvadoran ambassador to the United States. Sensing the president's distress and wishing to be helpful, the Salvadoran said, "Mr. President, you have helped our country so much, I think that we should try to help you with this problem. Give the mummy to us. I'm certain that Salvadoran science will be able to come up with the answer." The desperate Reagan acquiesced, and the mummy was secretly placed on a C-130 transport and flown to El Salvador. Three days later, the Salvadoran embassy informed the White House that the mummy was 3,567 years, 2 months, and 13 days old. A flabbergasted Reagan asked for details on the scientific method used by the Salvadorans. The reply came from the Estado Mayor. The cable read: "Mr. President. It took us a while to get the son-of-a-bitch to talk, but we finally got it out of him!"

My partner and I choked back the laughter and managed to remain stonefaced when the predictable punch line was delivered. Asked later why we had

not found the joke funny, we quietly told our disappointed Salvadoran contacts that we found human rights jokes to be in bad taste.

We were very serious about human rights.

Intervention

The success of the U.S. effort to end the human rights abuses of the
Salvadoran armed forces calls into question one of the core foreign policy
beliefs of liberal Americans of my generation: that it is wrong for the United
States to intervene in the internal affairs of sovereign foreign nations. Some
Americans seem to think that our attempts to influence developments in foreign countries are analogous to interfering in the domestic affairs of their
suburban next-door neighbors. I think what we did in El Salvador shows the
flaws in this line of thinking.

The Salvadoran armed forces were guilty of serious abuses and crimes
during the 1980s—this was accepted as a fact by the U.S. advisers with whom
I worked. These abuses strengthened the hand of the FMLN and, because of
the moral concerns of the American people, jeopardized the assistance that we
were providing to the ESAF.

One afternoon, during a long, rambling philosophical conversation, a
senior Salvadoran officer suddenly acknowledged that the ESAF was at least
partially responsible for the war and the violence. "We abused our power,
we abused the people," he said. The officer was well positioned to speak on
this point, because he himself was accused of precisely the kind of abuse he
was talking about: the FMLN's Radio Venceremos accused him of murder-
ing innocent civilians. I never doubted the veracity of this particular piece of
FMLN propaganda.

To prove his point about the ESAF's abusive behavior, the colonel suddenly turned to a group of civilian ESAF employees who happened to be
loitering nearby. "How many of you were at one time the victim of abusive
treatment at the hands of the Salvadoran armed forces or the security forces?"
he asked.[2] I was astonished when every one of the six or seven people present raised their hands. One gentleman described an encounter with a drunken
national guardsman who had held him to the ground and placed a cocked pistol to his head as his terrified wife and child looked on. The other civilians
present nodded knowingly, as if they were aware of similar incidents.

The fact that by 1986 these civilians felt comfortable discussing this in
front of a Salvadoran colonel and a U.S. military adviser was an indication

that things had changed for the better. Most journalists working in the country were reporting a dramatic decline in the number of death squad killings. During my time in El Salvador, I never saw a dead body in the streets—a sight that had been quite common in the early part of the decade. There had been a big change, and the United States was largely responsible for it. Every U.S. official in the country—including at one point a visiting Vice President Bush—had made sure the Salvadorans knew that the United States would not continue to support an armed force that systematically violated human rights. The dramatic decline in ESAF human rights abuses was the direct result of our efforts to influence and change Salvadoran military behavior—we had successfully intervened in the internal affairs of the Salvadoran military.

We had not necessarily changed the deep-seated values of the ESAF, of course. We had not somehow magically changed their hearts—we hadn't turned lions into lambs. From time to time the Salvadorans would slip up and we would get a reminder that attitudes from the bad old days were lurking just below the surface. One of my American colleagues recounted his first in-country meeting with Salvadoran army officers:

"Are you armed?" asked one ESAF officer.

"Yes," replied the American.

"Good. If anyone out there gives you any shit, just kill them," advised the Salvadoran, with a strongly implied, "Because that's what we do."

But because of our intervention the Salvadorans had to watch their steps. Some outside observers seemed to think that the American advisers and the Salvadoran officers were very chummy, and that this closeness must have hurt our ability to enforce our human rights policies. In most cases relations were friendly, but the Salvadorans knew that we were, in effect, their overseers, the ones who would turn them in if they committed an atrocity. This generated a certain amount of tension.

I felt this tension on the night that I served as the American duty officer in the Salvadoran military's 24/7 operations center. There was always an American in there keeping an eye on things. I felt very much like the overseer, and the Salvadorans on duty seemed to see me that way as well. On the night I pulled duty, the Salvadoran officers present were both badly wounded combat vets—one had lost an eye, the other an arm. They tried to rattle me by fabricating an intelligence report that an FMLN hit squad was en route to the operations center to get the American duty officer. It had been very important in SF school never to lose your cool in front of colleagues, and the training at Camp Mackall helped me out that night. Their little trick was a subtle reminder that even though we were working together, we were on two very different teams.

Critics of our human rights intervention claim that it was not really effective. Many point to human rights violations that took place late in the war. The 1989 slaughter of Jesuit priests at San Salvador's Universidad Centro Americana (UCA) is frequently used as evidence of the failure of our intervention. But even in this atrocity I found evidence of the positive results of our work: ESAF Colonel Carlos Armando Aviles violated the ESAF's code of silence by reporting the name of the Salvadoran officer responsible for the atrocity to MILGRP; that officer was eventually convicted and sent to prison. At the time, Aviles was the leader of the PSYOP section of the General Staff Headquarters. We had trained most of his staff, and he himself had been one of the star students in our counterinsurgency PSYOP course. I like to think that our emphasis on human rights paid off when he stepped forward.

Our intervention in the ESAF's human rights performance was, of course, part of a much broader U.S. intervention in the country. In El Salvador, our policy started from a very simple premise: that it was in the interest of the United States to prevent the Marxist-Leninist FMLN from shooting their way into power. We were prepared to intervene in El Salvador to prevent that from happening. The limited nature of our national interest in El Salvador put limits on the scope of our intervention. Our republic would not crumble if El Salvador fell, so we decided early on that the situation did not justify the direct use of U.S. combat troops. It would be advisers only, and no more than fifty-five.[3] Left to their own devices, the ESAF would have probably lost El Salvador to the FMLN, and U.S. security interests would have been seriously damaged. We were in El Salvador as part of a limited U.S. intervention designed to prevent that unhappy outcome.

Unlike many of the American critics of our actions in El Salvador, I saw no basic conflict between U.S. and Salvadoran interests. The Salvadorans wanted to live in a democratic country. They wanted their country to develop economically. The United States wanted the same things for El Salvador— not just because we are nice people, but because it is in our national interest for countries geographically close to us to grow more prosperous and democratic. Critics who accused us of denying the Salvadorans the revolution that they supposedly wanted and needed ignored the desires expressed by the Salvadorans in several national elections. They also ignored the dismal economic failures of Marxist Leninism in all corners of the Third World.

So I had no moral anxiety about helping out with our intervention. I felt good about what the United States was trying to do in El Salvador. But I had some serious misgivings about the way we were doing it.

PSYWAR

MILGRP did a good job providing the Salvadorans with the matériel and training they needed to prevent an FMLN victory. We used the influence that came with a $100 million annual security-assistance budget to force the Salvadorans to adopt morally acceptable human rights policies. And we helped prevent the FMLN from winning the war. But during my time in El Salvador, MILGRP failed to help the Salvadorans come up with an effective strategy to bring the war to a successful conclusion. I think one reason for this failure is the conventional military orientation of the U.S. officers who led our security assistance effort in El Salvador.

Conventional military strategy is the strategy for a World War II–style war — conflict between two heavily armed, high-technology armies. Conventional warfare is large-scale warfare involving divisions and corps — tens of thousands or hundreds of thousands of men maneuvering against each other using tanks and artillery, airplanes, and armored personnel carriers. The U.S. Army of 1986 was an overwhelmingly conventional institution. It was trained and equipped to face an attack of Soviet armored units in Europe. Unfortunately, expertise in this kind of war does not result in proficiency with the smaller-scale warfare waged by Third World Leninists. In many ways, proficiency in conventional warfare actually leaves the combatant at a disadvantage on the revolutionary battlefield.

While conventional warriors focus on the conquest of territory and the physical destruction of enemy forces, the revolutionary warrior in the Third World normally focuses on the political-psychological dimension. Starting from a position of conventional military inferiority, he essentially ignores conventional military concerns. He does not seek to hold territory, and he does not seek to engage in the kind of pitched, large-scale battles so familiar to the conventional warrior. The revolutionary warrior works in the shadows and seeks to capture the sympathy and support of the population. He uses the military tactics of guerrilla warfare. Military attacks are carried out only when they are judged to support the political-psychological objective. Conventional military men have trouble understanding this and often make the mistake of evaluating guerrilla military operations by conventional military standards.

Conventional soldiers see war as a battle for territory, but for the Central American revolutionary warrior, the only really important territory was the space between the ears of the average Central American citizen. The U.S. Army was staffed and led by conventional soldiers. The FMLN was composed of revolutionary warriors. In his May 1985 *Military Review* article, Colonel Waghelstein notes: "For both doctrinal and organizational reasons, revolutionary warfare goes deeply against the grain of the U.S. military. The doctrinal problem is that in the U.S. military there has always been a widely shared belief that military issues are and should be kept separate from political issues. The organizational problem is that the U.S. military is a high-technology, big unit military."[4]

While I was in El Salvador, the headquarters of the ESAF's Third Brigade in San Miguel was attacked by guerrillas. Infiltrators and a small group of hard-core assault troops managed to seriously damage the most important ESAF garrison in eastern El Salvador and to kill or wound many Salvadoran soldiers. We learned about the attack the next morning when we noticed the helicopters ferrying the wounded into the capital. The ESAF turned the incident into a public relations disaster by lying about the number of casualties and then getting caught at it by the press. The reporters simply went to the San Miguel casket maker and asked how many coffins the brigade had ordered that morning. The attack was big news in El Salvador: it was the lead story on all the nightly TV news programs and the headline of all the morning newspapers.

Shortly after the attack, I spoke with a U.S. adviser who had been working for a long time with a Salvadoran brigade in one of the country's most violent areas. He confidently dismissed the San Miguel attack as "completely insignificant militarily" and assured me that it did not signal a shift in the "military balance" in the area. The FMLN had merely "concentrated its forces" in order to stage "a spectacle" that "didn't mean anything."

From the purely conventional military perspective, my colleague was right. But he and many other MILGRP officers often seemed to forget that we were not involved in a conventional war. The San Miguel attack had sent a powerful message pulsing through El Salvador: the FMLN was not dead, and the ESAF could not defend against them.

The significance of attacks like the San Miguel raid was brought home to me when, later, a very distinguished and wealthy Salvadoran woman asked me, "Why can't our *maricón* army finish off that small group of Communist terrorists?" *Maricón* (homosexual) is among the most powerful of Spanish pejoratives. Attacks like the one at San Miguel seriously eroded ESAF prestige while bolstering the image of the FMLN.

The profound differences in approach between the FMLN and the U.S.-supported ESAF were clearly illustrated by the way the two opposing forces staffed the units that were charged with winning the battle for hearts and minds. While I was in El Salvador, we learned that in one province alone, the FMLN had more than one hundred people whose sole responsibility was psychological warfare directed at the civilian population. These operatives constantly circulated through the province doing good deeds and talking up the revolution. We assumed that similar efforts were taking place throughout the country.

The PSYOP efforts of our side were, in contrast, pitiful and revealed a lot about our approach to the war. Even here MILGRP concentrated on gadgets. True to our traditional military orientation, after grudgingly (and belatedly) admitting that something should be done about PSYOP, we threw money and technology at the problem. Instead of concentrating on the all-important substance of the message to be transmitted, we focused on the technology involved in getting the message out. We bought the Salvadoran armed forces a nationwide AM/FM radio network. We supplied sophisticated and expensive printing presses, and special airplanes that could drop leaflets and make loudspeaker announcements over FMLN positions. We spent millions of dollars on equipment for our Salvadoran allies, but we largely ignored what they were going to do with it.

What they did was waste it on uncoordinated, poorly thought-out, and sloppily executed propaganda campaigns. My partner and I had trained the operators how to execute effective campaigns, but the ESAF lacked senior officers who could effectively coordinate psychological operations against the guerrillas. The FMLN—operating without the equipment or the budget or the technology available to the ESAF—did a much better job at winning hearts and minds. In essence, the FMLN was winning the PSYOP battle because it had built an organization that generated superior intellectual firepower.

Shortly before I arrived in El Salvador, Joaquin Villalobos, the commander in chief of the ERP (People's Revolutionary Army—the most powerful and militant of the five FMLN factions), published an article in the Salvadoran journal *ECA*. Entitled "Views on the Current Status of the War," the article laid out in great detail the FMLN's analysis of the political, military, and economic situations.[5] Villalobos was particularly contemptuous of the conventional approach of the Salvadoran government. "Some of the thought of the government high command is extremely simplistic and reveals a very weak strategic vision," he wrote.

> It revolves around the assertion that the army has more battalions, more helicopters, more artillery. . . . It excludes the political and social factors and tries to establish and justify the following thesis, "We have an army that is so big, and the North Americans help us so much that we cannot possibly lose the war." . . . But history provides us with lessons. We must remember that: Somoza began his war with 7,000 troops . . . and lost when he had 15,000! Batista began with 30,000 troops . . . and lost when he had 70,000! The North Americans began their intervention with 3,000 advisers helping an army of 125,000 South Vietnamese . . . they lost when they had 500,000 troops supporting 1.2 million Vietnamese.
>
> In no case was the war won by the revolutionaries through the achievement of military superiority. These wars were won because the revolutionaries knew how to carefully use available military resources as part of the ongoing political struggle while bringing all of the people into the war. . . .
>
> In a popular war, the role of the military is not absolute. . . . Control of terrain is not in dispute. Our goal is to incorporate all of the people into the war . . . and to wear the enemy down. . . .
>
> Prospects for victory in the popular war lie in the correct and favorable combination of military, political, social, and international factors.

The magazine was openly available in El Salvador. *ECA*'s publisher offered to carry a rebuttal. My partner and I were fascinated by the piece and studied it in detail. We naively assumed that our ESAF students were doing the same, and that someone in the Estado Mayor was preparing an official rebuttal. We were wrong. The intellectual gauntlet remained on the ground. I was stunned to learn that none of the forty-five students in my PSYOP course had even bothered to read the article.

The war had effectively decapitated non-Communist El Salvador. Those wealthy enough to have received the kind of education needed to fight the battle of ideas had used their wealth and education to avoid participation in the war—some to escape completely from El Salvador. Even if they had stayed, they probably would not have been able to do much good; there was really no place for an intellectual in the Salvadoran armed forces. The ESAF just didn't recruit and develop thinkers the way the FMLN did. The war exacerbated the problem by encouraging a brain drain and diverting resources from education. FMLN terror tactics also played a role: Who would want to be a professor of political science at the Salvadoran Military Academy? Such a job would put a person high on the FMLN assassination list.

The contrasts between FMLN and ESAF personnel development were stark in other ways as well. I thought about this as I watched the cadets at El Salvador's military academy spend hours and days in grueling physical exercise: running around the campus carrying telephone poles, climbing ropes, enduring humiliating physical punishment. There was very little academic content in the four-year program. The ESAF recruited middle-class high school students, put them through four years of brutal basic training (with a sprinkling of academic classes), and graduated them into a system that placed no value on academic achievement or political work. The result was obvious in my class of forty-five would-be ESAF propagandists who had not bothered to read Villalobos's article, much less to rebut it.

The FMLN, in contrast, did have a system to develop and use intellectuals. And they used them to great effect. Miguel Castellanos was one example. His story provides some insight into the inner workings of the enemy organization.[6]

Born in 1949, Castellanos (whose real name was Napoleón Romero García) was a psychology student at the National University of El Salvador when he was recruited by the FMLN in 1973. He had been a student activist, and the Communist-controlled Unified Action Front had noted his leadership ability and speaking skills. He was approached by Atilio Cordero, a.k.a. Salvador Guerra, at one point the third- or fourth-ranking man in the FMLN's Popular Liberation Forces (FPL). Cordero invited Castellanos to join a secret study group at the university. The group was studying Marxist Leninism.

Cordero made progressively greater demands on Castellanos's study time. Castellanos resisted. When Cordero finally laid his cards on the table, Castellanos was surprised to learn that he had been dealing with a representative of the FPL. Cordero said that the FPL had selected Castellanos for recruitment as an active collaborator and told him to make a decision: Castellanos could be an academic or a revolutionary. If he chose to be an academic, Cordero said, the FPL would consider him an enemy of the people—there were no neutrals in the war. With mixed emotions Castellanos formally joined the FPL. Soon he came to fully embrace the Marxist-Leninist creed.

In 1974 the FPL was undergoing a fundamental reorientation. Originally involved in armed action, the group had decided to turn its attention to political-ideological work. At this early point in his revolutionary career, Castellanos wanted to join the FPL's urban commando team, but the FPL leadership had other plans for him. He was told to stay at the university and organize a new student group that would be under the direct control of the FPL.

In 1977 Castellanos told his family that he was going to Guatemala on business. Instead he went underground and became a clandestine operative. He stayed underground for eight years. At first he continued to work at the university, serving as the coordinator of FPL activity on campus. He worked out of a safe house and employed the cellular concept of organization: operatives of the FPL knew the identities of only the two or three others in their cell. Information was compartmentalized. Such cells and compartments protected the organization from infiltration and from the consequences of capture and interrogation.

His clandestine status gave Castellanos the opportunity to prove himself militarily; in other words, it gave him the chance to demonstrate his dedication to the cause by killing people. He led teams that killed two night watchmen in San Salvador (perhaps to steal their weapons). He also delivered "revolutionary justice" to a man in San Miguel who had decided to quit the revolution (while absconding with some of the revolution's money).

Castellanos's revolutionary career highlights the profound differences in orientation between the FMLN and the ESAF. Castellanos was selected and recruited because of his intellectual and persuasive skills. In his revolutionary career, military action took a clear backseat to political-ideological work. This same principle was applied throughout the organization. Castellanos explained:

By statute, the requirements for promotion to positions of high-level leadership [in the FMLN] are: high levels of revolutionary spirit, high levels of a spirit of sacrifice, profound love for the people, and operational ability. When it is seen that a militant does not really have military ability, he is told to concentrate on other areas, like management of the mass organizations, education, organization, propaganda . . . if someone does have military ability, he is allowed to specialize in military matters and he is given command of guerrilla groups. But whatever the case, the ideology and the ability to understand the party line are the fundamental requirements. Priority is given to political-ideo-logical development—military work should run parallel to it.

By 1979 Castellanos had been appointed the FPL's politico-military chief in the strategically important province of San Vicente. In July of that year, the Sandinistas brought down Somoza; revolutionaries throughout the region were encouraged and inspired by the victory. A group of younger ESAF colonels, terrified that the Communist contagion would spread from Nicaragua to El Salvador, overthrew the clumsy military dictatorship that had ruled El Salvador and—in an unsuccessful attempt to defuse the revolution—formed a "Military Revolutionary Junta."

With the Sandinista victory now in hand, Fidel Castro turned his attention to El Salvador. First, Castro insisted that the FPL and other insurgent groups consolidate under a unified military command; thus was born the Faribundo Martí National Liberation Front—the FMLN. "The Cubans came to be the agents," Castellanos said, "and Nicaragua the warehouse and bridge for the passage of solidarity [assistance] to the FMLN. Nicaragua, as a result of a decision of the Cubans, was converted into a base of operations for political, diplomatic, and logistical issues. The Sandinistas were to arrange how and by what means the arms would arrive to the FMLN and how they would be distributed among the various groups that had come to make up the Front." In San Vicente, Castellanos worked to recruit campesinos for FPL military units while continuing to build up the mass organizations.

In January 1981 Castellanos participated in the failed "final offensive" of the FMLN. Taking their lead from the successful 1979 insurrection of the Sandinistas, the Salvadoran Communists—with Cuban advice—decided to go for a quick victory through a series of bold military strikes that would spark a popular insurrection, bring down the government, and present the incoming Reagan administration with a fait accompli. The insurrection never got off the ground; many of the military strikes failed completely. Castellanos tried unsuccessfully to take the ESAF garrison at Zacatecoluca. The FMLN tried again in 1982 to launch an insurrection, although this time they didn't dare label it the "Ofensiva Final." Again they failed. The two failures led to a big shakeup in FMLN leadership and strategy.

That shake-up led in turn to a major crisis within the FPL that included an ugly murder-suicide: the FPL's leader ordered the murder of his deputy, whom he thought was getting too close to the Cuban overseers. When he was found out, the FPL's leader committed suicide. In the aftermath of this catastrophe, the FPL sent a delegation to meet with its principal international supporters to explain what had happened. From Managua, Castellanos traveled to Cuba, the Soviet Union, and Vietnam. In each country he met with key leaders of the Communist Party to explain how the FPL planned to recover from the disaster. The murder-suicide had planted doubts in Castellanos's mind; his tour of the Communist world deepened those doubts.

I met Miguel Castellanos in El Salvador in May 1986. Our PSYOP course included a block of instruction on Communist theory. We wanted to spice it up with something special, so we arranged for Castellanos to come in as a guest speaker. His class was entitled "Practical Application of Marxist-Leninist Theory in El Salvador." We never told the students beforehand that Castellanos was coming, fearing that advance warning might prompt some bitter and vindictive ESAF student to assassinate our guest speaker. We simply put "Guest Speaker" on the training schedule and let his appearance come as a surprise.

Meeting Castellanos for the first time was a bit unnerving. I was in uniform and felt distinctly uncomfortable as the observant revolutionary scanned my jacket, noting my rank and looking very carefully at my name tag. I worried that he might still be in contact with his old comrades. Castellanos told me that he hadn't met any U.S. Army officers. I laughed and told him I hadn't met any Communist guerrilla commanders. It was like one of those dramatic "East meets West" encounters in spy movies.

Castellanos spoke during each iteration of our PSYOP course. On each visit I waylaid him and learned a bit more about his career with the Communists and his reasons for abandoning it. There is still some disagreement about Castellanos's defection. Officially, the ESAF maintains that he defected from the FMLN. The FMLN claimed that Castellanos was captured by the ESAF and "broke" under torture. The *Miami Herald* quoted an unnamed military source as saying that he was captured by the ESAF but not tortured. I do not know the exact circumstances of Castellanos's withdrawal from the FMLN, but our conversations did provide some insight into the reasons for his ultimate change of heart.

The murder-suicide left a very bad taste in Castellanos's mouth. While the ideology called for selfless sacrifice and team effort, Castellanos noted that intrigue and blind ambition were the sad reality. Ironically, Castellanos's disaffection with Marxist Leninism was solidified by his grand tour of the Communist world:

With the experiences that I lived through in the war, and what I saw of the communist model in the countries that I visited, I came to be in disagreement with the Marxist-Leninist doctrine that forms the foundation of the FMLN. This doctrine consecrates violence as the midwife of history and maintains that in order to resolve social injustices, it is necessary to form a long-term dictatorship of the proletariat, a dictatorship, a form of government that exercises absolute power, that does not permit opposition, that denies all of the rights of the individual, that denies the people their religious beliefs. This I had seen and understood during my travels. It's one thing to visit the Soviet Union or Vietnam and have a translator explain things; it's quite another matter to go to Managua or Cuba where you can talk to people who share with you a history, a culture, a language. It's very different when you speak with Marxist Leninists in Spanish.

There is an old saying: "If you are not a Communist when you are twenty, you have no heart. If you are still a Communist when you are thirty, you have no head." Castellanos was twenty-four when he was recruited and thirty-six when he quit the revolution. I think getting older had an impact on his decision to quit. The lifestyle of a clandestine revolutionary seems attractive and exciting to a twenty-year-old. By thirty, the thrill is gone and thoughts turn to family, children, and stability.

I can write freely about Miguel Castellanos because he is no longer in danger. On February 16, 1989, urban commandos of the FMLN assassinated him in San Salvador. I was with the contras in the Yamales Valley near the Honduras-Nicaragua border when I heard of his death. When the Voice of America's Spanish-language service announced that a former FMLN commander had been gunned down in the Salvadoran capital, I knew right away that it was Miguel Castellanos who had been killed, and that the FMLN had killed him.

I worked with one other FMLN defector, but I must be more circumspect in writing about him because he is still alive. I'll call him Rafael. He was an FMLN military commander, a "trigger puller" who had racked up an impressive record of military strikes against the ESAF. He had been trained in Cuba and Nicaragua, and had killed a lot of people. His defection was potentially very useful for our side.

The ESAF wanted to use Rafael as an example. They wanted him to appear on television and radio to let other FMLN guerrillas know that he had defected, and that he was alive and had not been tortured. They wanted other FMLN guerrillas to follow his lead. I wanted him to help me with a training film that I was going to produce about PSYOP in El Salvador and to participate in the end-of-course projects of our students (some of which turned into real-world operations).

Unfortunately, Rafael didn't want to play. He was anguished by his defection. He had betrayed people who meant a great deal to him, people he had fought alongside under horrible conditions for many years. Rafael did not want to be humiliated in front of these people by serving as a puppet for the Salvadoran army. He didn't want words put in his mouth by the ESAF. But we needed his collaboration.

I was among the first group of American military officers to meet Rafael. He was very nervous in his initial meeting with us. But the fact that he did not hesitate to tell us about his reluctance to help with the ESAF's PSYOP efforts says something about the changed human rights practices of the ESAF: a few years earlier the ESAF might have killed him for his reluctance. When I met him, he was not really a prisoner. He had taken advantage of an amnesty granted to defectors who collaborated with the government. I interviewed him at an ESAF facility, but he was free to leave. His movements were limited only by the fact that he was in grave danger from the FMLN. He did not have to cooperate with us, but having betrayed the FMLN, it was obviously in his interest to stay on the good side of the ESAF and the gringos. But we put no real pressure on him, and I always assumed that if he had adamantly refused to cooperate, we would have simply backed away.

I was only a few years older than Rafael, and from the start we seemed to get along well. After our first meeting I scheduled a one-on-one follow-up. We had the chance to speak freely then, and I asked him to tell me his story.

Rafael said that he had been sixteen years old in 1979 when two of his brothers were killed by right-wing death squads. They had been involved in some sort of student movement. I had no way of knowing if they had been in a legitimate student group or in a front group like that of Castellanos's, but given what I had heard about the indiscriminate mayhem of 1979 El Salvador, I had no reason to doubt Rafael's claims that they were not involved in subversive activity.

Outrage and fear drove him to the FMLN. He started out as a low-level messenger, but because he demonstrated military skills he was given increasingly important leadership positions. Before my meetings with Rafael I had watched selections from captured enemy videotapes that showed him leading his FMLN troops in formation. It was obvious that he had real bearing, real command presence. Even on tape, it was obvious that he was in charge. After specialized training and briefings in Cuba and Nicaragua, he participated in daring attacks in San Salvador City. He told me that in preparation for one major raid, the Cubans and Nicaraguans had carefully built a scale model of the targeted ESAF air base.

In our conversations, Rafael's anguish was evident. He obviously was looking for a way to justify what he had done, a way to justify his defection. I asked him about the conditions in El Salvador that had driven him to the FMLN. Death squads, military government, hopeless poverty, no hope for peaceful change—it was a textbook description of the conditions that drive poor young men into Communist revolutionary movements. Then I asked him about conditions in El Salvador in 1986. This question gave Rafael pause. He thought for a while before acknowledging that things had indeed changed. The fact that he was still alive was an indication that things had changed in the ESAF. And José Napoleón Duarte—not some general—was president. Though the poverty was as bad as ever, it could no longer be said that there was no peaceful avenue to change.

Rafael told me that while he was in the movement he had been unaware of the changes that had taken place in El Salvador. The leadership of the FMLN deliberately (and for good reason) kept their troops in the dark on such matters, and deliberately painted a very bleak and deceptive picture for them. Duarte was presented as a puppet of the army and the U.S. imperialists. Troops were told that death squads still operated and that the ESAF would torture and kill them if they surrendered.

Here, obviously, was the justification for Rafael's defection: things had changed. I told him that I could understand and sympathize with his decision to take up arms in 1979, but in light of the changes that had taken place in El Salvador, armed struggle was no longer justified, no longer necessary. I told him that just as he had done the right thing in 1979, he had also done the right thing in 1986 when he had abandoned the violence. It was now his duty to explain this to his former comrades who continued to risk their lives because of the lies of their FMLN commissars. Our conversations seemed to have a big impact on Rafael. I don't think that anyone in the ESAF had ever spoken to him in these terms. He agreed to work with us on PSYOP projects.

Rafael was afraid that the words the ESAF would put into his mouth would make him look stupid, so I suggested that he write his own scripts. He liked this idea and for several weeks drafted and redrafted his own PSYOP campaign. From time to time we sat down together to look over his work. We both laughed when I pointed out that I would have to edit some of his language: he was still referring to the ESAF as "lackeys of the imperialists" and "running dogs." Old habits die hard.

Rafael helped me with my training film and starred in a campaign designed by our students to encourage the members of his FMLN unit to follow his example. We prepared leaflets, radio announcements, and loudspeaker messages (for broadcast from special PSYOP airplanes). Soon Rafael's old unit was being bombarded with a multimedia ESAF PSYOP campaign. In the messages Rafael explained his change of heart and encouraged his troops to turn themselves in.

Because PSYOP campaigns target intangibles like morale and esprit de corps, it is always difficult to measure their effects. In an ideal world, we would run a few radio spots, throw a few leaflets, and then watch the guerrillas see the light, throw down their weapons, and march down from the mountains with their hands up. Unfortunately, it doesn't ever happen that quickly. We merely hoped that our operation would succeed in planting some doubt in the minds of the troops in Rafael's old unit. Maybe some of them would decide not to return to the revolution after their next Christmas leave (yes, even FMLN guerrillas took vacations). Even if it just planted some doubts, the campaign might lead to more FMLN desertions or defections. More desertions meant less bloodshed.

It was becoming obvious that a lot of FMLN members were getting tired of the war. One afternoon, my partner and I received a radio call from the MILGRP telling us that "something interesting" had taken place near San Miguel in eastern El Salvador. We were instructed to get out to the airport for a flight going east. When we got to the airport and I saw the small, French-made helicopter that was going to make the trip, I was sure that there wouldn't be a seat for me. The MILGRP commander, Col. James Steele, was there, as were a couple of Salvadoran officers and my immediate superior, Maj. Pedro Arbona. Counting the number of seats and including one for the pilot, we were obviously one seat short. I was sure I was going to get bumped . . . until I learned that we weren't taking a pilot.

Colonel Steele was a cavalry officer who, it was said, sometimes wore his cav boots (with spurs) in the embassy. He ruled MILGRP with an iron fist (there may have been no other way to do it), and members of the unit really feared him. His last comment in radio transmissions was usually, "Make it happen!" with an implied, "or else." Due in part to the frosty, suspicious atmosphere that pervaded MILGRP, we had had very little contact with him—and we were grateful for this. We even did our best to steer clear of him when jogging on the enclosed and guarded quarter-mile track that we used for exercise; this was a bit awkward when there were only three of us running.

Steele told me to jump into the backseat of the chopper. To my amazement he climbed into the pilot's seat and began to fire up the engines. I didn't know that he could fly that little French helicopter! He took us on an exciting low-level flight through eastern El Salvador. Later, at the brigade headquarters in San Miguel, he asked the Salvadoran commander if he would like a lift back to the capital. Machismo notwithstanding, the Salvadoran demurred: "No, thanks. I think I'd rather take the bus." A wise man.

It was an interesting day. Zipping along at treetop level across the FMLN-dominated territory and carrying a CAR-15 assault rifle (a cut-down version of the M-16), I was getting my first look at the real consequences of the war: the countryside was full of downed bridges and power towers. Peasant homes flew white flags in a desperate effort to stay out of the fight.

At the San Miguel Brigade Headquarters we met the objects of MILGRP's interest: three young fellows who until very recently had been members of the FMLN's People's Liberation Army. What was interesting about them was their method of disassociating themselves from the movement. After finding out that the FMLN wouldn't allow them to quit the revolution, the three of them had taken matters into their own hands. They pumped bullets into the head of their sleeping FMLN commander and then approached the ESAF and turned in all of their unit's equipment and weapons.

We didn't want to encourage this kind of mayhem (El Salvador already had more than its share of violence), but we did want to encourage guerrillas to turn themselves in. Soon the ESAF was embarking on a campaign to let other guerrillas know about the defection of the three fellows in San Miguel (without too much emphasis on the assassination of their commander).

My conversations with Castellanos and Rafael and my observations in San Miguel revealed a way out of El Salvador's violence. Rafael was typical of the very important midlevel military leaders of the FMLN. His case was an example of how national-level reforms could have a direct and devastating impact on the guerrilla movement. Properly approached, leaders at Rafael's level could have led troops like the three murderous defectors down from the hills. Unfortunately, our team (the ESAF and their MILGRP advisers) did a very poor job of delivering news about the reforms to the FMLN.

In targeting people like Castellanos, we should have publicized glasnost and perestroika. We should have been telling them that the Soviets and the Eastern Europeans were abandoning key elements of the ideology that the FMLN was still trying to impose on El Salvador. Certainly there was an element within the FMLN that was completely aware of the failure of socialism and was merely using Marxist Leninism as a vehicle to personal power. But I think many in the FMLN were still true believers in the synthetic, godless religion of Marxist Leninism. We should have been telling these people that their Kremlin high priests had lost the faith.

Shortly before my departure from El Salvador, an American colleague and I took Miguel Castellanos and Rafael out to lunch. At this point Castellanos was moving around with a small platoon of ESAF bodyguards. After we departed the Estado Mayor, security guards in tow, we randomly selected a restaurant (so that nobody could have had advance word of our lunch plans). Miguel, Rafael, my colleague, and I all rode in our armored sedan.

Going out to a restaurant in El Salvador was always a bit of an adventure. There was always the possibility that you wouldn't make it to dessert. The ride through the streets of the city would set the mood. Mindful as always of the ambush threat, we drove fast with guns at the ready, ignoring stop signs and red lights. We always took a table that allowed us to keep our backs to the wall and our eyes on the door. On our laps we would have our handguns, concealed (barely) in the "*mariconera*" gun-purses that had become the de rigueur fashion accessory for the armed and dangerous set. People seemed to know who we were, and sometimes, in an effort to stay out of a potential mealtime massacre, other customers would ask to be seated at tables far from ours.

Having former FMLN members as our guests made lunch even more interesting. In an attempt to make conversation, my American colleague asked Rafael if he had ever carried out operations in San Salvador City. Rafael smiled sheepishly and said, "Well, yes, I did. As a matter of fact, I once fired several rocket-propelled grenades into the United States embassy. I hope you won't hold this against me!" Guerrilla war makes for strange lunch partners.

In August 1986, my mission in El Salvador ended and I returned to Fort Bragg. Soon I found myself back in the stifling, mindless bureaucracy of the stateside peacetime army. No one in my unit was interested in what I had been doing in Central America. Instead they seemed contemptuous of those of us who had been "goofing off down there." My fellow officers seemed to resent the fact that my group had escaped from the mindless tedium in which they wallowed.

Not that they really wanted to go "down there" themselves—they had careers to build and tickets to punch, and El Salvador wasn't on the pathway to high rank and military success.

The army personnel system's attitude toward our work was confirmed when Hugh, my partner in El Salvador, went to Washington to review his file. Hugh was an Air Defense Artillery officer who was coming up for promotion to major. He later told me that the personnel officer had flipped through his evaluation file, noting a steady sequence of good evaluations for Hugh's artillery assignments. Then the officer got to the evaluation of our work in El Salvador. We were very proud of these ratings—they described our direct contributions to the fight against world Communism—but the personnel officer appeared puzzled. He squinted at the evaluation as if he had found something mildly offensive. "Well," he said, "I guess this won't hurt you too much." He then went back to flipping through the file. Sadly, from the army's perspective, Hugh's time in El Salvador would apparently have been much better spent as an assistant operations officer doing training exercises in an Air Defense Artillery battalion in Fort Bliss, Texas.

Concern in my unit was firmly focused on improving the battalion's "statistics"—increasing the percentage of our troops who had participated in the myriad training activities mandated by the army. El Salvador seemed a million miles away as I watched our soldiers waste their time on such meaningless projects as learning how to respond to a nuclear attack. I tried to ignore as much of this nonsense as I could and to stay in touch with what was happening in Central America.

One afternoon, as my poor troops frantically polished the forty-five-year-old wooden floor in preparation for the much-feared annual general inspection (preparation that had taken absolute priority over the few "real world" projects we had), I read through the daily pile of message traffic that arrived from around the world. I kept a lookout for messages from El Salvador. One unclassified report caught my eye: it dealt with an FMLN ambush. At the bottom of the message I saw, among the list of those wounded in the attack, the name of one of my students.

Roxana had impressed me as a most unlikely participant in an ugly guerrilla war. This gentle, quiet, frail girl seemed completely out of place in discussions of guerrilla war and Marxist Leninism. A civilian employee of the Salvadoran armed forces, she was a social worker in one of the Salvadoran army battalions. Her job had been to handle the many psychological and emotional problems that the long war brought to the young campesino soldiers in her battalion. Machismo and the aloofness of the Salvadoran officer corps prevented the unit's officers from handling such morale problems. She had become completely devoted to the despondent young soldiers she counseled. When the Salvadoran army had decided to get involved in PSYOP, they sent Roxana and some of her colleagues through our course.

At several points in our program students were required to present briefings on operations that they had planned. The reports usually began with a short description of the overall purpose of the operation and a perfunctory explanation of how it related to the Salvadoran war effort. Roxana's presentation began with a fiery and sincere exposition on the need to win the war and bring democracy to El Salvador. She was really dedicated.

News of her wounds only accentuated my unhappiness with my work at Fort Bragg. While people like Roxana were struggling against Communism in Central America, I was playing silly games in North Carolina. At around this time, some friends in MILGRP initiated an effort to bring me back to El Salvador on another six-month mission. I wanted to go, but one of my superiors wanted me to stay at Bragg and help make him look good in upcoming training exercises. Far too many people in the military bureaucracy were more worried about their ratings and their promotions than the war effort in Central America. I had always derived a great deal of personal satisfaction from my military service, but I was getting tired of working under a hierarchy that sometimes seemed more interested in bureaucratic battles than in the fight against Communism. I knew it was time to start thinking seriously about getting out of the army.

CHAPTER 5

MAKING MOVIES

A Highway for Yoro: scene 1, take 1. ¡Acción, por favor!

BEFORE I GOT OUT OF THE MILITARY I made a few more trips to Central America. My assignment to the much-maligned PSYOP battalion had turned out to be a stroke of luck. If I had gone to a Special Forces battalion, I probably would have been involved in the boring and routine task of conducting basic training in Spanish for Latin American soldiers. The PSYOP assignment opened the door to more unusual and interesting projects, including a brief and bizarre stint as a motion picture director.

As part of our efforts to put the Salvadoran army on the path of righteousness, MILGRP was producing training films. The films were intended to be both entertaining and educational. We wanted to improve the Salvadoran army's morale, tactical proficiency, and respect for human rights. Somehow, in the midst of a war, and using essentially amateur producer/directors, we were able to produce some high-quality and entertaining products.

When the PSYOP course ended, I was asked to stay in El Salvador to produce a thirty-minute video that would explain the essential points of psychological warfare to senior Salvadoran army officers. The video would let them know about the PSYOP resources available to them and how best to employ those resources. I had about a month to do the job. My only prior experience with film production was my work on a short movie for a high school English class.

Hugh had returned to the United States, and in order to comply with MILGRP's "never travel alone" rule, his place in the rental car and at restaurant tables had been taken by a sullen bodyguard from the Salvadoran Special Forces. Most GIs involved in overseas conflicts deploy in the company of thousands of fellow Americans. My experience in El Salvador (especially during that last month) was very different; I was almost completely on my own.

For the technical aspects of the video project we had contracted the services of a small and somewhat spooky video production company. This outfit was staffed by a bunch of Chilean Christian Democrats who had decamped to Venezuela after Pinochet ran them out of Chile. Christian Democrat connections in Caracas had led them to Salvadoran President José Napoleón Duarte's people and to media work in El Salvador, and thus to my project. Their attitude toward me, an officer in the gringo war machine, was marked by a not very subtle ambivalence, but somehow we managed to get along. The Chileans helped with the filming and editing; the script writing and the direction were up to me.

A short documentary of this type is not difficult to produce. First I wrote a script. After it was approved, we did the audio narration; for this we contracted a professional narrator and used the sound studios of the ESAF radio station.

While writing the script I had made some preliminary notes on the kind of images I wanted for each portion of the video. Most of the required images were available in the ESAF's video library. We rummaged through the archives until we found suitable clips, which we then spliced onto the narrator's soundtrack. For those portions of the video that required new filming, we arranged for the necessary actors, locations, and video crews. (Rafael was one of our stars.) The new images were spliced in along with the archival clips. Finally, appropriate music was selected and mixed with the narration and video. After a little polishing, the video was done. I'm not sure if this is the technique taught at film schools, but it worked for me.

Producing a video in the midst of the civil war presented special problems and difficulties. A colleague of mine, for example, was working on another film and needed to shoot some scenes depicting events in an FMLN-controlled village. For authenticity he wanted lots of FMLN graffiti on the walls. Unwilling to take the ESAF film crew into enemy territory, he decided to use a village near the capital that was not under FMLN control. The problem was that the selected village did not have the needed pro-Communist graffiti. There was only one thing to do. . . . The poor villagers must have been astonished when my colleague and a platoon of ESAF soldiers showed up one morning and started to paint "¡Viva el FMLN!" (Long live the FMLN!) on the walls of the town square.

My own experiences with video-perplexed Central American villagers came later, in Honduras. As part of my battalion's participation in exercise Solid Shield '87, I was ordered to produce a thirty-minute video that would explain to the Honduran people what the U.S. Army construction battalions were doing in their country. There were a lot of rumors about this phase of the military exercise program—most people thought we were building an invasion route to the Nicaraguan border. My superiors wanted me to make a movie that would explain what our soldiers were really up to: they were just practicing roadbuilding, and were doing it in an area where the Honduran peasants desperately needed roads. Because Solid Shield '87 was designed to test our battalion's ability to operate in the field, I was ordered to do the video production under field conditions.

My entire battalion had deployed to La Ceiba, a nice little city on the north coast of Honduras. After the preliminary script writing, archival video selection, and sound work, we headed for the construction site to do some filming "on location." I needed to interview some of the Honduran peasants who had benefited from the project.

The road was being built in the Honduran province of Yoro. I had been there before and knew it to be one of the country's most isolated and underdeveloped provinces—the kind of place where you could tune across the entire AM dial on your car radio and hear only static. Our battalion was based on the Caribbean coastal plain, which fronted a spectacular range of jagged mountains that could be described as Alpine if it were not for their lush tropical greenery. Some areas of this mountain range had not yet been explored or mapped. Yoro was directly on the other side of the mountains; getting there required an expedition. With great gusto (which stemmed from a burning desire to get away from the bureaucracy that we had imported with us from Fort Bragg) I set about putting together a small Video Expeditionary Force. I rented a Japanese-made pickup truck and selected a small team of soldiers—two cameramen, a mechanic (for the truck), and a Honduran soldier (for security). We packed the pickup with equipment and provisions and set out for a weeklong mission to the lost province of Yoro.

The Yoro expedition was typical of the kind of jobs I did during my short but charmed army career. We were doing something for which no manuals had been written, and we were given a lot of leeway by superiors who realized that the only way to get the job done was to leave us alone. When we arrived in Yoro, we were a self-sustained, quasi-independent, five-man international military video team.

The American combat engineers working in the Yoro area were living at a large base camp called Oso Grande (Big Bear). Located in a cool pine forest and occupied mostly by laid-back, congenial American National Guardsmen on their two-week annual training tours, Oso Grande had a definite "summer camp" feel about it. The food was good and we liked the atmosphere, so I arranged for us to stay in the camp.

We used up a lot of videotape shooting scenes of bulldozers at work, happy American and Honduran soldiers digging ditches, and so on. The really fun part, however, was our series of interviews with the Honduran peasants who were benefiting from this Cold War windfall.

The peasants (the much softer Spanish word is *campesino*, meaning "country person") had had almost no contact with the outside world. I have always found Central American campesinos to be generous, friendly people, but getting the Yoro peasants to consent to interviews in front of a big, threatening-looking video camera turned out to be difficult. The few who would agree to be interviewed invariably froze when faced with the camera. Instead of voicing effusive praise of the benefits of the new road (as they really did off camera), they would stand stiffly and speak in monosyllables. The result appeared to be an interview coerced at gunpoint:

"Do you like the road?"

"Uh . . . (nervous look; eyes shift back and forth) . . . yes."

Obviously, we had to turn on the charm and warm these people up. At first we thought that the Honduran soldier who had accompanied us would be helpful in this effort, but that didn't work out. I'm not sure whether it was because he was just not very charming or because the campesinos didn't like Honduran soldiers, or maybe they just preferred to talk to the Americans. It was probably a combination of these factors. The Honduran soldier was quickly returned to his role of security guard, and I took on the role of chief interviewer.

To get our subjects warmed up for the interview, we talked casually to them for a while and explained the purpose of our project. We shared our army rations with the kids who gathered around. The rations helped, but the real ice-breaker was the Polaroid.

We had discovered on previous visits to the Honduran hinterland that the campesinos were absolutely crazy about having their pictures taken. Nowhere in the world was a Polaroid photograph more appreciated. Their attitude toward the Polaroid cameras reflected their isolation from the modern world and the huge gulf of misunderstanding that separated them from us. At first we didn't realize why the Polaroid pictures were such a big deal. But during a visit to one small village I noticed that one of the women started to cry when the images of her children began to appear on the Polaroid film. Slowly we came to understand that these people had never had their pictures taken; the Polaroid shots that we were so casually leaving behind were the only pictures that these parents would ever have of their children—our little photos were destined to become cherished family heirlooms. With this in mind we became less casual about taking the pictures.

Back at Fort Bragg, we ordered the production of a "background frame" for the snapshots. It featured the Honduran and American flags along with an inscription that read: "Thank you for the courtesy and kindness shown to us during our visit to your town. Please accept this little gift as a token of our friendship and gratitude." We always asked the adults for permission to take the pictures, and we always tried to get one or two GIs in the scene. After a picture had developed, we would glue it to the frame and present it to the head of the household. The people really loved those pictures.

I'm always a little uneasy about foreigners with gifts descending on poor Third World villagers, but I felt good about the Polaroids. I think it was a nice thing to do, and I think it won us some friends. It certainly helped warm up our interview subjects. After seeing themselves on film once, many of them turned positively loquacious. After a little pep talk, I would seat myself behind the camera and say something like, "Tell me about what the new road has meant to you." That was enough. Soon we had numerous interviews with a broad and representative sample of public opinion in the area of Puentecitas, Yoro, Honduras. Our mission accomplished, we packed up our little truck and headed back to our battalion's coastal base camp at La Ceiba where we did the editing and put the video together.

One final note on how we got our program on the air. When people hear the word *propaganda*, they usually think of sneaky, clandestine operations. But there was nothing covert about this project. After getting all the necessary U.S. and Honduran approvals in Tegucigalpa, Panama, and at Fort Bragg, I simply took the video to several Honduran television stations. I presented myself openly as a captain in the U.S. Army and explained the purpose of the project, then asked to purchase thirty minutes of airtime at the standard rate. We quickly reached agreements with each station, and the video went on the air.

CHAPTER 6

THE FOREIGN SERVICE AND EMBASSY TEGOOSE

Croquet? We're really going to play croquet?

THE WAY I GOT INTO THE FOREIGN SERVICE shows how itinerant my life was during the 1980s: I was still at Fort Bragg in early 1985 when I signed up for the Foreign Service written exam. Knowing that I would be in Panama on the exam date, I specified that I wanted to take the test there. I was in Honduras during the week before the exam—I studied for the test on the plane that took me from Tegucigalpa back to Panama City. I may owe my passing grade to the fact that I arrived in Panama exhausted from the Honduras mission. On the night before the exam I slept soundly for twelve hours; I have never been more rested for a test. The exam was administered amid palm trees and tropical humidity on the campus of the old Canal Zone Community College. A few months later, back in the States on a visit to Fort Bragg, I flew up to Washington for the oral portion of the exam.

I was in El Salvador when I got the word that the orals had gone well— the State Department sent me a thick packet of application forms and asked me to write a short autobiography. I was too busy to spend much time on it. I wrote my Foreign Service autobiography one quiet Sunday afternoon while seated at poolside at the San Salvador Sheraton; the atmosphere was just right for such a task.

Months passed while the State Department carried out a security investigation. Men in dark suits visited my hometown neighbors and asked about my childhood. A security officer from Washington came down to Fort Bragg to interview me. By the summer of 1987 the government had apparently decided that I wasn't a Soviet agent. I was in Honduras when they offered me a position in the Foreign Service. I left the army in November 1987 and immediately went to Washington for the State Department's orientation course.

Washington was a cultural breath of fresh air after years of Fort Bragg and Central America. My classmates were a congenial and interesting group. The rather bizarre lifestyle that we had all just adopted seemed to create a special camaraderie in the class. Most of us had abandoned other careers for this, and all of us had agreed to accept assignment anywhere in the world. We were all going overseas, but none of us knew where in the world we were going.

The course had a light, no-pressure curriculum. One of its objectives was apparently to help us integrate into the collegial network of the Foreign Service. This was called "bonding." On two occasions during the course we were sent out to bucolic convention centers for two or three days of intensive bonding. After four years of the cold and prickly army, I found the warm and fuzzy approach of the Foreign Service amusing and refreshing.

Most days in the course were spent listening to lectures from representatives of the various State Department bureaus. We were frequently sent from our Rosslyn, Virginia, classroom to the State Department's Washington headquarters for visits to the working offices. We weren't being trained to do anything specific—the assumption was that the examination process had selected people who already had the necessary skills. The course was designed simply to orient us to our new work environment and responsibilities.

I managed to get into some interesting arguments, most of them about Central America. On the first day of the course we were all asked to stand up and give a brief description of our personal backgrounds. When my turn came, I announced that I was "proud to have served as an adviser in El Salvador." This threw down the gauntlet, in a sense, and stirred up a series of debates on Central America policy that went on intermittently (sometimes incessantly) for the rest of the course. The discussions were sometimes intense, but they were always friendly and collegial, and I enjoyed them. I found it amusing that with no real change in my opinions I had gone from being the class leftist in SF school to being the class rightist in FS school.

Early in the course we were provided with a list of about forty-five available overseas posts. Since there were forty-five people in our class, it seemed obvious that one of us was going to each of the posts on the list. Most people join the Foreign Service with visions of going to exotic, elegant foreign places—Paris or Singapore, perhaps. Our list contained many such desirable postings, but it also included places like Ciudad Juárez, Mexico; Lagos, Nigeria; and Port-au-Prince, Haiti. Of course we had known that these places were possible postings, but now we faced the real possibility of actually having to live in them for two years. As they say, it focuses your attention.

The list provoked some good-natured gallows humor. On one of our getting-to-know-you bonding excursions, a psychologist asked each of us to stand up in front of the group and reveal something personal that we had not yet told the class. In a very somber and serious manner, one classmate rose and, looking down at his shoes, confessed that he had a very serious, incurable, and debilitating disease . . . that prevented him from *ever* being able to serve in Ciudad Juárez, Mexico. The shrink was not amused, but the rest of us found this hilarious. As assignment day drew near, we organized a pool. Each member of the class selected his "worst post on the list" and placed the selection along with five bucks into a hat. Whoever was sent to that post got the loot. The pot was eventually split between three heroic FSOs: two en route to Port-au-Prince and the other to Lagos.

Throughout the course we had waited with trepidation for the announcement of our assignments. Some people were going a little crazy fretting over their future. The procedure used to make the announcements brought the anxiety to a peak. On the appointed day, the personnel officers arrived in our classroom with a box of small flags. We had known that this was going to happen, and many of us had studied up on the flags of our most likely destinations (we had been given the chance to express our preferences). One by one, classmates were called to the podium and presented with the flag of the country to which they had been posted. Most people were very happy with their assignments—by and large, the China specialists went to China, and so on—but a few whimpers could be heard as the assignments were announced.

I watched with growing apprehension as all of my "preferred" posts—Havana, Lima, Bogotá, and a few others—were handed out to colleagues. Finally, my name was called and I was handed the very familiar blue-and-white flag of the Republic of Honduras. I was going back to Embassy Tegucigalpa, this time as special assistant to Ambassador Everett Ellis Briggs.

This was a big surprise because "Tegoose" had not been on our list. It was also a bit reassuring, because immediately prior to the assignment selection process I had engaged in a no-holds-barred argument about Central America with the chief of the personnel office. After that, some classmates thought that I would never be allowed anywhere near Central America. I was happy that they were sending me back.

I arrived in Honduras on March 11, 1988. My introduction to Foreign Service social life was a "welcome aboard" cookout that had been organized to greet the newly assigned officers. I approached the event with some nervousness, worried that the army had not prepared me for the social niceties of the diplomatic service. I was temporarily relieved when I found an old army buddy (who had also joined the Foreign Service) at the party. My anxiety returned, however, when the hosts confirmed all my Foreign Service stereotypes by announcing that we were all going to play croquet. I thought they were kidding. They weren't. I quietly asked my ex-comrade-in-arms what to do. He advised me to follow his lead and "fake it." I didn't win, but I survived.

My first days at the embassy were a strange mix of operational tasks and social events. On my first or second day in the office we received a secure telephone call from Washington. After speaking intently and taking notes for several minutes, the officer who had taken the call hung up, smiled at me, and said, "What timing! Your first week on the job and we have a war on our hands!" The Sandinistas had sent troops into Honduran territory, and the embassy was shifting into high gear.

Plans for a U.S. military response to the Sandinista incursion quickly began to gather steam. One of the first State Department telegrams that I worked on dealt with the dispatch of U.S. troops to Honduras. My role was to carry the draft telegram from the embassy up to the ambassador's residence at midnight to get his approval. It was all very dramatic.

There were tense staff meetings in which big decisions were made. I was so new to the embassy and so unsure of my role in the scheme of things that I didn't know whether I belonged in any of these meetings or not. After an amazingly short period of telephone conversations, consultations, and telegram sending, a brigade from the 82nd Airborne Division was on its way. I accompanied the ambassador to Palmerola Air Base, my former home, where he was briefed by the military commanders and where we later watched our troops parachute into Honduras for training exercises intended to scare the Sandinistas back into Nicaragua. Even though this seemed like a wild way to start work at the embassy, it turned out to be only a prelude to even more dramatic events.

A couple of weeks after the military deployment, on April 7, 1988 (less than a month after my arrival in Tegoose), an angry mob of about one thousand screaming Hondurans stormed the embassy and sacked our annex building. The riot had been sparked by the arrest of Juan Ramón Mata Ballesteros, a key figure in one of the Colombian drug cartels who had set up shop in Tegucigalpa. His arrest and deportation raised constitutional issues in Honduras. Many believed that provisions of the Honduran Constitution were violated when he was handed over to U.S. justice. Agitators used these constitutional questions to whip up a crowd. Some of Mata's henchmen were also almost certainly involved in setting off the riot, as were radical leftists (who hated us as a matter of principle).

I was with some colleagues in a restaurant near the embassy when the riot started. As always, we had a walkie-talkie with us; the routine radio chatter provided the background noise for our dinner conversation. Around seven o'clock we heard the marine at Post 1 (the main entrance to any U.S. embassy) announce that a demonstration was under way. That was not an unusual event; no cause for real alarm. Dinner continued. About fifteen minutes later we heard the marine—this time with urgency (but no panic) in his voice—tell one of our security officers not to approach the embassy because the crowd had turned violent. He then reported that the embassy was being hit with Molotov cocktails. That was the end of dinner.

We emerged from the restaurant to find normally sleepy Tegucigalpa in pandemonium. In the confusion, a couple of embassy family members ended up in my car. I had to get them safely to their homes before figuring out what to do next. As we drove through Tegucigalpa, we skirted the fringes of the crowd that was by now encircling the embassy. Menacing groups armed with clubs and sticks appeared along our path. The radio chatter on the embassy frequency grew increasingly worrisome. We learned that with the embassy surrounded, the new command center was at the ambassador's house, which was located on the side of a mountain overlooking Tegucigalpa and the embassy. After leaving the family members safe in their homes, I headed up the hill.

From the ambassador's residence we could look down on our embassy. There were fires all around it, and I believe we could hear the roar of the crowd. Through our radio system we were in touch with the marines and the embassy officers who were still inside the besieged buildings. It appeared that the main building (the chancery) was relatively secure; the large, six-story annex across the street was bearing the brunt of the attack.

One American officer had been working in the annex building when the crowd arrived. The building was on fire, but it would have been suicidal for an American to try to get out through that crowd. Mob psychology had kicked in—the crowd resembled sharks in a feeding frenzy. As the smoke got thicker, the officer trapped inside had to use the emergency air tanks of the building's pre-prepared safe haven.

At the residence we were frantically trying to get the Honduran authorities to come to our rescue. Their failure to respond to the attack became a major scandal. As we waited, we had to listen to our colleague's calm voice from inside the burning building. At this point we did not know when or if the Honduran police would respond. All we knew was that they had taken no action yet.

Sometime around nine o'clock, our defense attaché, Col. Mark Jones, and a Honduran colonel who had been his dinner guest swung into action. Both were in uniform. We were still trying to reach the senior officers of the Honduran government to get them to order a rescue that should have been automatic. The defense attaché and the Honduran colonel jumped into a car and sped off to the fire station nearest the embassy, where they found the firemen sitting around "waiting for orders." The two officers gave them some very blunt and direct orders, and the fire trucks started moving.

I think it was about nine-thirty or ten o'clock when the Honduran authorities finally came to our assistance. The riot police showed up and fired a few shots in the air, and the crowd evaporated. By that time, millions of dollars in damage had been done. Several Hondurans in the crowd had died from gunshot wounds. (The shots had come from within the crowd. It seems the riot's organizers were intent on acquiring some martyrs—one way or another.)

Around eleven o'clock the security officers said it would be all right for the ambassador to go to the embassy. Accompanied by security guards carrying shotguns, we jumped into an armored sedan for the drive down the hill. Chaos reigned at the embassy. Hundreds of helmeted Honduran riot policemen, each carrying a big gray riot shield, lined the sidewalks. Stragglers from the riot and curious passersby milled around outside the still-smoking annex building. The streets were filled with burned-out cars, most of them carrying diplomatic license plates.

Inside the mission, a thin cloud of residual tear gas hung in the air and stung our eyes. It seemed that just about everybody was carrying a shotgun.

The ambassador went to see the brave crew that had stayed in the embassy during the riot: the marines, Political Counselor Don Johnson, and the man who had been stuck in the burning building, Gene Szepezy. Gene was covered with soot and looked like he had just puffed on an exploding cigar.

There was a tense midnight staff meeting in which we tried to analyze the situation. Around one-thirty in the morning we started to disperse. By then the rioters had all gone home to bed. Tegucigalpa was as sleepy as ever.

Violent aftershocks continued for some time. The next day bomb blasts rocked Tegucigalpa, but the embassy itself was not hit. The government had declared a state of emergency, and Honduran army battalions were in the street. The government had also taken over all the radio stations, and they were all broadcasting an ominous, nonstop medley of patriotic music. The embassy was very tense. At one point I was standing in the ambassador's office with my back toward the window. Looking up from his desk, the ambassador advised me to stand away from the window. He was worried about snipers.

Some particularly memorable images and stories come to mind when I think of those tense days:

- On the night of the riot, a senior embassy officer was hosting a cocktail party attended by some high-ranking members of the Nicaraguan democratic resistance—the contras. When news arrived that the embassy was under siege, some of the contras—only half-jokingly—suggested sending a few of their boys down to disperse the crowd and stop the riot. At the time I'm sure it seemed like a ridiculous notion, but considering the catastrophe that followed, perhaps the embassy should have taken them up on their offer. Just imagine the resulting headlines: "Besieged U.S. Embassy Rescued by Contras." What a public relations coup that would have been for the resistance!

- On the morning after the riot, as we sifted through the rubble, Paul Novak, one of the security officers, recovered an American flag that the mob had pulled out of the consulate and tried unsuccessfully to burn. Paul had been up all night. In the wire service photo that flashed around the world you could see fatigue and sadness in his face as he cradled our flag in his arms and carried it to safety.

- In the weeks immediately following the riot, every Thursday (the riot had been on a Thursday night) our radical Honduran opponents would attempt to mount follow-up demonstrations in memory of their "martyrs." Some of these demonstrations had the potential to cause real damage, and the Honduran government's willingness to defend us was uncertain. Every week, as the hour for the demonstration approached, the embassy would take on an Alamo-like atmosphere. Most of the embassy personnel would be sent home early. Our by-now-augmented marine detachment would be in battle dress with helmets and flak jackets and shotguns. The officers who stayed on in the embassy would listen to radio reports on the activities of the crowd—on one of these Thursdays it really looked as if they were coming to get us. On that day the embassy felt like a bunker.

- During one of these Thursday afternoon sessions a delegation of European parliamentarians was visiting the embassy. Apparently they had insisted on coming, riots notwithstanding. So of course they got stuck in the embassy just as it looked as if the crowd was going to surround it again. During the period of real danger we stashed the delegates in a relatively secure area of the building. At the earliest safe opportunity we put them back on their bus and sent them back to their hotel. Some of them looked quite disgruntled as they waddled down the embassy corridor past heavily armed marines, with traces of tear gas still in the air.

- The Americans who suffered most during the riot were undoubtedly the embassy family members. Every embassy household (there were hundreds) had an emergency two-way radio, and most of the families were listening to the disturbing radio messages from the people who were trapped inside the embassy.

- Even at a distance, family members suffered. For the first time in my Central American career, my parents were really frightened. About two days after the riot, a call from home reached me in the embassy's political section. My worried mother was crying over the long-distance line. It was a very tough time for all.

- Most Hondurans seemed to be stunned and horrified by the event. In the days after the riot we received many calls and telegrams expressing sympathy and sorrow over what had happened. People sent flowers. The ambassador assembled our bewildered Honduran employees and delivered a much-needed pep talk.

After things settled down a bit, I acquired a small house on the outskirts of Tegucigalpa. Life in Tegoose was very pleasant, but it had its bizarre elements.

We had twenty-six channels of U.S. cable television. I could eat microwave dinners from the embassy commissary and watch live reports of snowstorms and traffic jams in Denver while, just outside my window, rag-clad Honduran children struggled to carry large bottles of polluted water to their squatter shacks adjacent to my U.S.-style suburban neighborhood. In some ways the USA was very near, but in others it seemed a million miles away.

There was an enormous and very diverse U.S. presence in Tegucigalpa. Large numbers of American military personnel were in town, and we also had the world's largest Peace Corps program. There were a lot of reporters. The Totem Bar and the Maya Hotel served as social centers for a too-large group of young Americans who somehow managed to get along with each other in spite of profound differences in political and professional orientation—some of the social events seemed to be meetings of the Peace Corps, the War Corps, and the Press Corps.

Tegoose was a very strange place. I liked it very much.

The author with students at the Colegio De La Salle in Huehuetenango, Guatemala, summer 1979.

Destroyed armored vehicles in Managua, Nicaragua, June 1981.

Graduation day, Special Forces Qualification Course, spring 1983. The author is at far left.

Visiting a Honduran village, 1985.

En route to San Miguel, El Salvador, to interview insurgents, late 1985.

On a break from instructor duty in El Salvador, 1986.

The author with Enrique Bermudez (a.k.a. Comandante 380) at the Strategic Command headquarters in Yamales, Honduras, 1988. An Air Log chopper is in the background. Bermudez was assassinated in Managua on February 16, 1991.

The author at Banco Grande on the border between Honduras and Nicaragua, 1988. Nicaragua is on the other side of the Coco River.

The author interviewing contras who have just crossed into Honduras from Nicaragua, 1988.

Contras at Banco Grande, 1988.

Contra field commander CH-5 at Banco Grande, 1988.

Contras, 1988.

Contra commanders at Banco Grande, 1988. Some wear clothing taken from Sandinistas.

Contra graduation formation at the Military Instruction Center near Yamales, 1989.

Contras at a helicopter landing zone awaiting resupply, 1988.

Saying good-bye to the contras in Yamales, 1989.

CHAPTER 7
EMBATTLED FARMERS

By the rude bridge that arched the flood,
Their flag to April's breeze unfurled,
Here once the embattled farmers stood,
And fired the shot heard round the world.

—"Concord Hymn" by Ralph Waldo Emerson

Whenever any form of Government becomes destructive of these
Ends, it is the Right of the People to alter or to abolish it.

—Declaration of Independence

MY INVOLVEMENT WITH THE CONTRAS began in August 1988 when several of the senior officers at Embassy Tegucigalpa went back to the States for home leave and consultations. The four-person State Department office that handled resistance matters was already seriously understaffed. When the chief of that office, Tim Brown, was tapped to serve as acting deputy chief of mission, Chargé John Penfold asked me if I would be willing to forgo leave in order to fill in for a month as liaison officer to the Nicaraguan democratic resistance. When I was presented with the offer, another senior official in the embassy privately warned, "Don't become a player in this unless you really want to be one." I wanted in. Thus began my stint in the Special Liaison Office as a diplomatic representative to the contras. "Welcome to the nut house!" was the reaction of one of the embassy's other participants in "the project."

The Special Liaison Office (SLO) of Embassy Tegucigalpa did exactly what its title indicated: it carried out the special liaison that existed between the Nicaraguan democratic resistance and the U.S. embassy. I'm sure that the SLO raised the suspicions of those in search of skullduggery, but as I frequently pointed out to visiting Americans, our work was very similar to that carried out by the political or economic sections of U.S. embassies around the world: maintaining contact with local leaders, reporting to Washington on developments, and explaining U.S. policy to local interlocutors.

Of course, working with the contras was a far cry from the normal diplomatic routine. On the one hand, it was very exciting, very satisfying work. I have roared across the savanna of the Honduran Mosquitia at dusk on a motorcycle borrowed from the leader of rebellious Nicaraguan Miskito Indians. I have had the adventure of literally going to the field in search of information needed by my government, and the satisfaction of coming home with the goods. On the other hand, my work put me in direct contact with one of the most frustrating and difficult foreign policy situations the United States had faced since World War II. It was not always easy to be a point man for a controversial policy that, in its later stages, seemed designed to destroy an organization filled with courageous people fighting for the values that form the essence of our own national identity.

Yamales

By August 1988 the resistance had endured about six months without U.S. "lethal assistance"—six months, that is, without U.S.-supplied bullets. Under legislation passed by Congress in the spring of 1988, the U.S. Agency for International Development (USAID) was providing only nonlethal U.S. assistance to Honduras-based resistance personnel: food for the troops and their families, uniforms for the troops, and medical care. For the several thousand troops who remained inside Nicaragua, USAID provided the Honduras-based commanders with Nicaraguan currency (cordobas) at the rate of about one dollar per day per combatant. Resistance couriers carried the cordobas to the troops inside Nicaragua.

By the time I became involved, the cutoff of U.S. assistance had forced most of the contras out of Nicaragua and into Honduras. They were down, but they were not out. They had been driven to "sanctuary," but they were holding together as an organization. Many officials in the embassy and Washington seemed surprised by the contras' cohesion—I think they had expected them to fall apart quickly when U.S. lethal assistance was cut off. But they didn't fall apart.

The vast majority of the troops were living in one isolated valley in a region known as the Las Vegas salient. The valley itself was known as Yamales. Some ten thousand troops and thousands of their family members were encamped in an area about six miles long and two miles wide. The troops lived as members of some twenty-five distinct units, each with its own separate base camp. A six-man General Staff operated from a headquarters site in the valley.

After receiving my temporary assignment from the chargé, I decided that I should jump right in and spend some time in Yamales. The valley was one hour away from Tegucigalpa by helicopter, or six hours away by precarious road. Most gringos working in the valley chose to commute by helicopter from Tegucigalpa. Yamales was austere and extremely uncomfortable for those unaccustomed to life in the field, and few Americans were willing to make overnight visits. But I realized immediately that the only way to find out what was happening was to spend some time living with the resistance. Day trips would not be enough. The helicopters that we used had to be back in Tegucigalpa before dusk; it's hard to develop contacts—and credibility—in a guerrilla army if you have to be home before the streetlights come on. So I gathered up what remained of my army field gear and told the chargé that I would be back in a few days. This was a big adventure: I was going into forbidden territory. The border zone was strictly off-limits for embassy personnel. Even the embassy's military officers were prohibited from going there.

The helicopter dropped me off at the Strategic Command site just as a meeting of the Council of Commanders of the Northern Front was about to begin. Fortunately for me, senior resistance political leader Enrique Bermudez (a.k.a. Comandante 380) had hitched a ride on the helicopter from Tegucigalpa; we talked during the flight, and he agreed to introduce me to the commanders. At this point, Bermudez was the only contra I had met.

While they were informally called a lot of things (contras, freedom fighters, mercenaries, and other names), the official title of the group I was visiting was the Nicaraguan Resistance Army–Northern Front. The Spanish acronym we used was ERN-N. Two other smaller armed groups were also fighting the Sandinistas: Atlantic Coast Indians were grouped together in an organization called YATAMA (a Miskito-language acronym for "Free the Motherland") and the Nicaraguan Resistance Army–South (ERN-S) carried out an independent and more limited campaign from Costa Rica. YATAMA and the ERN-N were nominally unified at the political level through their representatives on the seven-man Political Directorate. All of these groups were generically referred to as the Nicaraguan resistance, or (using the Spanish acronym) "RN."

The Council of Commanders meeting was a good place to start. Soon after climbing out of the helicopter I found myself walking into a crowded tent filled with contra field commanders. Scanning the faces in the crowd (faces that stared back with benign curiosity at the unknown gringo), I thought they looked the part: they really looked like Hollywood's version of Latin guerrillas. Cigarette smoke filled the air. The members of the council were all in uniform. Almost all of them had sidearms; several carried submachine guns. Longer hair and beards accentuated the difference between this group and a conventional army. They wore a wide variety of hats. All of the commanders used noms de guerre. The key leaders sat at a table; the other members of the council sat on a low bench that made them appear to be on their haunches, evoking the image of a tribal council.

I was surprised by the easy manner in which the commanders accepted my presence. Bermudez simply informed the group that I was a friend from the American embassy and that I would be observing the meeting; they got right down to business.

In the year that followed I attended many such meetings. American officials had easy access to the RN. It was generally a very open organization, and we were paying the bills. I found it easy to build friendly, productive relationships with contras of all ranks. I was helped a little by my military background—early in my initial conversations I would let slip the fact that I had been in the army. It was a useful icebreaker, and it helped me to establish a little common ground with my RN interlocutors.

The Yamales Valley is about seven miles from the Nicaraguan border. One small dirt road with a few side branches ran down the center. Like much of Honduras, the valley was seriously deforested—campesinos in search of firewood had denuded the hills. From the air, the valley terrain appeared oddly artificial. It looked lumpy, like a collection of large, grass-covered ski moguls.

The resistance troops lived in improvised huts built from scavenged bits of wood, black plastic sheeting, and ponchos. The regional commands looked like strange little nomadic settlements. Each formed a separate and distinct community with its own hierarchy and history. Like military units everywhere, the battalions formed their own distinct little worlds. A visitor encountered organizations, not mobs; an army, not refugees. If the commander was away from the unit, the duty officer was summoned to greet the visitor. Armed sentries provided security, but most of the troops in Yamales did not routinely carry weapons. The *comandos* (as the soldiers were called) could sometimes be found playing baseball—the favorite sport of Nicaraguans. Commanders tried to hold classes, but training resources were limited. A centralized training facility regularly offered courses for junior officers and troops.

The contras in the valley led a very Spartan existence. Much of the day was occupied with the necessities of life: getting clothes cleaned, hauling USAID-provided food back to the unit's mess hall, and gathering firewood and water. American visitors to the valley almost invariably commented on the difficult living conditions. "How can they stand it? I'd go nuts!" was the usual remark. The answer was cultural: The people living in the Yamales Valley in 1988 and 1989 were Nicaraguan campesinos; they were used to a hard life in the countryside. Most U.S. Americans probably *would* go nuts after a time in the Yamales Valley, but the people living in the valley were not U.S. Americans.

The contras were religious people. Many of the regional command base camps included small churches that had been improvised from sticks and bits of plastic sheeting. Nicaraguans have a special reverence for the Virgin Mary, and many of the contra combatants I met wore rosaries around their necks. There were no Catholic priests in Yamales. Occasionally a Honduran priest would go out to the valley to perform baptisms and marriages, but the contras had to get by without regular access to clergy. I was told that Assistant Secretary of State Elliott Abrams had tried without success to get some American Catholic priests to go down to minister to the contras. As I mentioned earlier, a crucifix fashioned from an M-16 bullet—the contra cross—was the symbol of the resistance movement. Enrique Bermudez joked that the contras had tried to make the crosses out of Soviet AK-47 bullets, but somehow they just didn't come out right.

There were also Hondurans in the valley. The resistance lived on previously undeveloped land owned by Honduran farmers. Most of the commanders had an arrangement with their landlords to provide some kind of compensation—sometimes the troops would help with farm tasks. While many contra opponents tried to portray the resistance as an army of occupation that had displaced and irritated the Honduran campesinos of Yamales, I did not find this to be the case. The most severe criticism I was able to uncover came from a Honduran woman who was unhappy that some contras had knocked over her fence.

In fact, the Hondurans in the valley openly sympathized with the plight of their contra-campesino neighbors. Relations between the Yamales Hondurans and the resistance were excellent. The resistance doctors routinely provided free treatment to ailing Honduran neighbors. Resistance commanders made sure the troops behaved themselves. In coordination with Honduran military authorities, liquor and beer sales in the valley had been banned. While Hondurans in Tegucigalpa frequently complained about crimes supposedly committed by the resistance, most of the complainers had never even seen a contra; I got the feeling that the xenophobic Hondurans were using the resistance as a scapegoat for the crime wave in Tegucigalpa. It is always easier to blame your social problems on foreigners.

The dirt road at the base of the valley was, in effect, "Main Street Yamales." I spent many days hiking along that road, visiting units and talking to people along the way. From dawn to dusk, it was traversed by a steady stream of young contra troops engaged in a variety of official chores and off-duty activities. Most were busy hauling heavy loads of supplies (big bags of beans, and of rice) back to their units from the distribution center set up by USAID. Troopers en route from their units to the warehouse would often come jogging down the road alone or in small groups, occasionally in military formation. Asked why they were running, the young combatants would answer that they had to stay in shape so that they would be ready when the time came to get back into the fight.

The road was also something of a shopping mall. Honduran and Nicaraguan merchants hawked cheap sunglasses, hats, soda pop, and other items from little stands along the way. Some of the merchants were Hondurans from nearby Trojes or Danli; others were Nicaraguan refugees trying to eke out a living. I made friends with a couple of the merchants and would occasionally pause at their stands to chat and drink a soda or eat an orange. It was a good way to keep in touch with the sentiment of the civilians who lived and worked in the valley.

After a few months of working with the contras, I started to recognize many of the individual soldiers. One afternoon, I was at the far northern end of the valley when I came across two teenage contras who normally worked at the Strategic Command Headquarters (which was located several miles away). They looked unusually dapper, and it was obvious that they were not hauling beans or playing volleyball that day. When I asked them what they were up to and why they were so far from their usual haunts, they sheepishly replied that they were en route to a certain regional command where they had met a couple of good-looking girls.

I was surprised to learn that most of the contras rarely left the valley to visit the nearby Honduran towns. They did get into Capire (the only town actually in the Yamales Valley—referred to jokingly as Managuita, or "Little Managua"), but when I asked about visits to Las Trojes, the usual response was an incredulous look. For many of them, going to Las Trojes was about as possible as a trip to Paris. A visit to Las Trojes required money and civilian clothes, and most of the contras had neither. I got the impression that the campesinos felt comfortable in the valley surrounded by their brothers in arms, but were quite wary of venturing into that foreign country called Honduras.

Young Warriors: Contra Demographics

While Sandinista supporters almost invariably described the contras as mercenaries or Somoza's National Guardsmen, these labels did not accurately describe the people I encountered in the Yamales Valley in 1988 and 1989. The vast majority of the resistance personnel were young campesinos. This demographic detail is the single most important fact about the Nicaraguan Resistance Army. It contradicts almost everything the Sandinistas and their supporters said about the contras, and it is itself a stunning indictment of the Sandinista regime. It was also almost completely overlooked by most American observers.

Late in 1988, the U.S. Agency for International Development asked Bob Gersony, an expert on conflict and refugees, to evaluate its humanitarian assistance program. Unlike other USAID officers in Honduras, Gersony spent a significant amount of time living in the field. He studied the resistance to determine who they were, what they needed, and how well USAID was meeting their needs. Aside from coming up with many recommendations for improving USAID's performance (adding certain vegetables to the diet, improvements in medical care, administrative procedures, etc.) he produced a report on resistance demographics. Here is what he found:

70 percent of the contras were under the age of 24

27 percent were 24–35 years old

 3 percent were older than 35

64 percent reported no formal education

23 percent reported having 1 year or less of education

13 percent reported having 2–5 years of education

97 percent identified their principal occupation as farming

The great majority described the location of their homes as rural farm villages.

Gersony's report substantiated what I had observed in the Yamales Valley: the Nicaraguan Resistance Army was an army of peasants. It was not an army of Somoza's National Guardsmen; when Somoza left Nicaragua in July 1979 most of the contras had not yet reached their fourteenth birthdays. It was not a mercenary army; the only compensation the troops got was the daily ration of rice and beans provided by USAID. If they were mercenaries, they came very cheap.

I think the demographics of the resistance were beyond the comprehension of most Americans. Lacking a peasant class ourselves, it is difficult for us to understand peasants. This lack of understanding is exacerbated by the tendency of many Americans to take a very one-dimensional view of foreign societies. Let's face it, the average American probably has a very vague conception of Nicaragua, perhaps seeing it as a small, poverty-stricken Hispanic country "somewhere down there."

Outsiders had a tendency to see the Nicaraguans as an undifferentiated group of Hispanics, but the society was in fact much more complex, with significant divisions based on class and race. I found it a cruel irony that American liberals—the group that fancies itself the sophisticated champion of the downtrodden—in effect aligned themselves with the city-dwelling whites of the Sandinista Front, and against the dark-skinned rural campesinos of the resistance. The racial factor in the Nicaraguan war should not be underestimated. More than once I heard myself described as a *chele* (white guy) by contras who meant no insult but didn't know that I understood their slang.

The peasant factor was, in a sense, the reason for the war. One afternoon a senior contra commander and I stood on a hill and looked down at a large formation of contras. This particular commander was a brooding, serious, menacing person—difficult to approach and not given to chitchat. Nor was he impressed by visiting gringos. So I was a bit surprised when he suddenly turned to me with a sociological question.

"Do you know anything about campesinos?"

I knew that I needed to respond quickly. I might not get another opportunity to connect with him. My answer came from the Peace Corps.

"Yes, I think I do."

"Well, what are they like?"

I told him what friends in the Peace Corps had told me. The Central American campesinos were very set in their ways, very reluctant to change, very difficult to organize or mobilize. They were people bound to the land, farmers who farmed the way their fathers and grandfathers had done.

"That's exactly right," he replied. "But look, we've got fifteen thousand of them with us now.[1] All of them were sufficiently angered to leave their homes and take up arms. Why did they do that? The Sandinistas obviously did something terribly, terribly wrong."

Resistance Sojourns

After my temporary summer assignment in the Special Liaison Office ended and the embassy was back at full strength, my bosses decided that I would continue as a liaison officer on a part-time basis. Two or three times a month I would break away from my other duties in the embassy and hitch a ride out to Yamales on the USAID helicopter to spend two or three days with the ERN. Even when I couldn't get away, I had frequent contact with resistance commanders who were based in Tegucigalpa or were passing through the city.

In Yamales, my mission was almost always the same: keeping a finger on the pulse of the resistance. I kept a cot in the corner of one of the tents at the Strategic Command Headquarters. I ate the same food that the contras ate, and after a time I came to feel quite at home in the valley. I looked forward to escaping from the bureaucratic routine and found the contras more pleasant company than many of my embassy colleagues.

The visits to Yamales were great fun: an opportunity for adventure and exploration, a chance to trade pinstripes and wingtips for blue jeans and jungle boots. I usually traveled alone, often taking satisfaction in being the only U.S. representative in the Yamales Valley. I enjoyed the independence and the sense of being as close to the issue as an American official could get.

Some days I would hike through the valley with a backpack, stopping in to visit the various regional commands. On arrival, I was sometimes offered a homemade beverage called *pinol*. It was nasty-looking stuff, and the improvised container was usually something that might have served as an oilcan in a previous life. But pinol was important to the campesinos, so much so that Nicaraguans call themselves *pinoleros* (roughly, "drinkers of pinol"). So I always managed to push fears of disease to the back of my mind and gulp some of it down.

The Nicaraguans were proud, but they could also be self-deprecating, and a national obsession with poetry had made them introspective as well. They told me of another, slightly pejorative nickname: *mucos*. Muco is a breed of cattle that has a reputation for stubbornness, they explained. Once a muco decides to cross a field, there is no deterring it. The nickname seemed to capture very well the contras' dogged persistence.

Meals at Yamales consisted of the USAID-provided rations of rice and beans, and occasionally a piece of meat or chicken. The food was served without knives or forks; everyone used large corn tortillas to scoop it up. Americans always had trouble estimating the proper ratio of tortilla to rice and beans. The contras would always have just enough tortilla to consume the entire portion of food on the plate, but visiting gringos almost always ran out of tortilla before eating all of the rice and beans. Meals were followed by strong, dark Nicaraguan coffee heavily laced with lots of sugar. I used to joke with the contras that henceforth I would always use more sugar in my coffee. Dinner would be followed by long conversations with commanders and troops. Clouds of cigarette smoke filled the tents as contras talked of the history of the movement and their hopes for Nicaragua.

I found the contras to be very warm, friendly, and open people. If anything, they were too open, too trusting. They were good hosts who always seemed to be genuinely happy to have an American in the camp. Sometimes I felt that the ERN looked upon me as some form of human good-luck charm—visible, living evidence that the great power to the north had not completely forgotten them, evidence that Washington still cared.

Sympathy for the Cause

I decided early on to be as straightforward as possible with the contras. When you are dealing with people who are wrapped up in a passionate struggle, there is the temptation to try to build bridges to them by casting yourself as a sympathizer. I decided to provide a more forthright explanation for my interest in the movement. It may seem undiplomatic, but after getting to know the senior leaders, I made it clear that my visits to the valley were not the result of my personal sympathy for their cause. I told them that while I did personally feel sympathy for what they were trying to do, I was in the valley in an official capacity to look out for the interests of the United States. The ERN leaders invariably responded positively to this approach. I think they appreciated the honesty. I got the feeling that they were sick of transient gringos bubbling effusively about their "sympathy for the cause."

Working with the resistance involved a constant effort on my part to avoid emotional involvement. I think that anyone who can deal with a group like the Nicaraguan resistance for a prolonged period without feeling human sympathy has no business being there in an official capacity. You cannot report accurately on human events if you have no human feelings. At the same time, I think that a U.S. official who becomes excessively sympathetic—to the point that he loses sight of his mission (protecting U.S. interests)—should be taken off the project.

But this was emotionally charged work. Halfway through my tour, one of my main contacts in the resistance—Comandante Aureliano—was assassinated in Tegucigalpa by Sandinista agents. I was in the Yamales Valley with his comrades when they received the news of his death. Soon after that a colleague and I took a resistance officer to lunch in a Tegucigalpa restaurant. He was still clearly shaken by Aureliano's assassination—his hands were unsteady as he tried to eat his lunch. In another meeting one of the comandantes broke down and started to cry when talking to one of my colleagues. This was highly unusual for the very macho contras, and a clear reminder of the emotional toll that the war was taking.

Throughout my tour I regularly visited the resistance hospitals and rehabilitation centers where mangled and crippled people much younger than I embodied the human costs of the struggle. Every time I went to the valley, I spoke for hours with simple campesinos passionately committed to liberating their country. It was hard to stay emotionally detached. I always reminded myself that I was not the resistance's representative in the U.S. government— I was a U.S. government representative to the resistance—an important distinction easily lost in the emotions of guerrilla war.

My training as a Special Forces officer helped me to remain objective. The SF instructors had encouraged a very cold-blooded, detached approach to "the guerrilla force." Some Q course classes dealt specifically with the demobilization phase—the phase when the U.S. government has decided that it is in our interests to see the guerrillas disarmed and demobilized. We were told to use our ingenuity to come up with ways to carry out the demobilization— guerrilla sentiments be damned. In one exercise, a student came up with what we later called the "ballistic demobilization technique." The Gs were being recalcitrant about demobilization, so the advisers pretended to sympathize. A weapons maintenance class was organized. As soon as the guerrillas removed the bolts from their weapons, the U.S. advisers stepped back and a prepositioned machine gun violently demobilized the G force. The young captain who designed this maneuver was perfunctorily criticized by the instructors, but it was obvious that his ingenuity and ruthlessness were, to a certain extent, admired. By the time I got to the contras I was well prepared to be very cold-blooded in my dealings with them.

Calculations of the U.S. interest determined our every move. There were some variations in how the Americans involved in the contra project saw those interests, but I think we were all in agreement on some basic notions. All of us saw the Sandinistas as dangerous, expansionist allies of the Soviet Union. U.S. military exercises in Honduras served as a constant reminder of the potential (albeit remote) for direct U.S. military involvement. I think there was also a consensus that we would have no real peace in Central America as long as the Sandinistas remained in power. Most of us saw the contras as a palatable way of dealing with the Sandinistas, a way of dealing with them that avoided involving U.S. troops in a bloody, controversial (and perhaps unsuccessful) war.

Many Americans opposed our aid to the contras out of fear that it would lead to another Vietnam. Ironically, most of us who advocated aid to the resistance did so because we saw it as a way to avoid having to send U.S. troops into Nicaragua. We too sought to avoid another Vietnam. In all my dealings with the resistance, I always had it in the back of my mind that if somebody had to fight and die in Nicaragua, it was far better for the United States if Nicaraguans were doing the fighting and dying. I didn't want to see U.S. soldiers involved in Nicaragua, and I didn't think that such a move would have served the national security interests of the United States. I thought we had other, better options. We had the contras.

Others in the embassy had more personal reasons for favoring the contra option. One senior officer said that he didn't want to wake up some morning to find that his teenage son had been drafted to fight in Central America. That was our nightmare: a rambunctious Sandinista regime spreading chaos throughout the isthmus, El Salvador falling, and an American president facing two unappealing options: capitulation or the use of U.S. troops. This fear may seem ridiculous now, but when we were fretting about this scenario the Berlin Wall was still up, and the Soviet Union was still a real threat.

In terms of the U.S. interest, as long as the Sandinistas were in power, I could not see how we would benefit from a demobilization of the contras. I realize that the U.S. national interest was not the paramount concern for many critics of the Reagan policy—some seemed to be more concerned about the interests of the Sandinista regime. Many others chose to ignore the nasty realities of this world. They based their criticism on "higher" moral concerns and opposed the policy simply because they didn't like war. Those of us who worked with the contras didn't like war either, but unlike the private citizens we served, we had direct responsibility for protecting U.S. interests in an area where our enemies were not at all reluctant to employ armed force. In the July 17, 1989 edition of the *New York Times*, Assistant Secretary of State Elliott Abrams observed that "critics have the luxury of invoking whatever concept they find useful in the struggle to resist a vigorous United States foreign policy, but policy makers live a tougher life." Philosophers (and Sandinista supporters) could find myriad reasons to disband the contras, but looked at strictly in terms of U.S. interests in 1988, such a demobilization was difficult to defend.

So for the first six months of my involvement with the resistance, during the final months of the Reagan administration, our goal was to preserve the resistance as an option for the incoming administration. This clear and unambiguous objective helped to bring coherence to our efforts and justified the extraordinary measures that we sometimes took to help keep the force together. We all worked with the satisfying assurance that we were doing something important and useful for Uncle Sam; we wanted to be able to present the incoming president with a full set of options regarding Nicaragua, a set of options that included an armed resistance movement.

Glasnost, Perestroika, and the Contras

When I joined the State Department in November 1987, many people in the government, including me, did not believe that Mikhail Gorbachev was going to put an end to Soviet aggression. During the course of my training in Washington (November 1987–March 1988), however, Gorbachev visited the United States, and a number of prominent conservatives (among them Jeane Kirkpatrick) began to point out that perhaps Gorbachev's glasnost (openness) and perestroika (economic restructuring) were precisely what the United States had been waiting for. National Security Council Document 68—the blueprint for the Cold War—had been assigned reading in the Foreign Service orientation course. It provided a useful reminder of what it was that we were hoping to achieve. The Cold War wasn't over yet, but maybe Gorbachev's reforms were the first signs that victory was at hand.

It was interesting to watch my colleagues in Tegucigalpa struggle with the rapidly evolving global situation. Many were convinced that glasnost was just another "dirty commie trick." Colleagues who had served in the Soviet

Union were especially pessimistic and cynical. During this period a member of the policy planning group of the State Department's Latin American Bureau came down to visit. He was an expert on the region who had been brought into the department to provide outside views and strategic wisdom. I knew him from my army days. We sat poolside at Tegucigalpa's Maya Hotel and talked about Central America. I was amazed to learn that he was not thinking about the Central American consequences of Gorbachev's heresy. He was so bogged down in the minutiae of day-to-day problems in Central America, and so thoroughly stuck in the Cold War mindset, that he had not even considered the implications of perestroika for Nicaragua. I think a lot of people in Washington were stuck in the same analytical trap.

The strategic issue was really very simple: If the Sandinistas were agents of an aggressive and powerful Soviet enemy, then Nicaragua was an important place for the United States. If the Soviets were no longer quite so threatening and aggressive, then Nicaragua diminished in importance for us. I do not think that Nicaragua in itself was ever of any real importance for the United States. It became important only when the Sandinistas made themselves an extension of an empire that we saw as evil and strategically dangerous. If the evil empire was no longer evil, then the Nicaraguan war became an anachronism, an annoying and unimportant vestige of the Cold War, a fly in the soothing ointment of Gorbachev's glasnost, an impediment to the creation of a kinder and gentler world.

The new global reality made it more difficult to be a U.S. representative to the resistance. Most of the combatants were blissfully ignorant of the changes that were taking place in the world, but some of the more senior political types understood what was happening. One afternoon in Yamales, a visiting Miami-based resistance politico engaged me in a discussion of Gorbachev and glasnost. I told him that I honestly thought there might be something to it—that after forty-five years of waiting the West might be seeing the start of change.

My interlocutor was clearly disturbed by my analysis. I got the impression that he had not heard a gringo speak this way before. Rather than being happy that Cold War tensions might finally be easing, he was worried about the implications for the contras. Almost everyone in the resistance had pinned their hopes on a renewal of U.S. lethal assistance. The politico clearly recognized the significance for the contras of the possible change in the U.S. worldview. In terms of U.S. assistance, the fat lady wasn't singing but it sounded like she was clearing her throat. Privately, as I walked through the dusty Yamales

Valley in that dry season of 1988–89, I pondered glasnost and wondered if I was walking through a dustbin of history.

While to us the world seemed to be changing, nothing had really changed for the resistance. Their world was Nicaragua, and there was no evidence that the winds of change had reached their oppressed little country. Their dependence on us placed them in a very precarious situation. Sometimes it seemed hopeless. It was sad to see well-motivated people—people who were fighting for the things the United States stands for—struggling against such great odds.

Wilfredo is a very quiet, calm person—in many ways the antithesis of Hollywood's stereotypical "frito bandito" Latino guerrilla leader. When I worked with the resistance, he was in charge of a hideous patch of mountain jungle known as the Bocay. Ten days' march from the relative luxury of Yamales, the Bocay was the home of a small, dedicated group of resistance soldiers and civilian supporters. There were no roads to the Bocay. It was an isolated, difficult, boring place to live. Wilfredo was the commander out there.

Because the bulk of the resistance force was in Yamales, I only occasionally got out to the Bocay to talk to Wilfredo. He was a modest man, but over the course of our visits I managed to find out some of the details of his long and distinguished resistance background. He was one of the founding fathers of the famous Salazar units. Named for the revered leader of Nicaragua's coffee growers' association who was assassinated by the Nicaraguan State Security Service in November 1980, the Salazar regional commands were widely considered the most effective and most "guerrilla" of the RN units. Wilfredo carried painful scars from his long war, including a serious spinal wound that had left him paralyzed for several months. He was not yet completely recovered from it, but he had returned to duty after the contra high command decided that they needed him to lead ERN-N forces in the inhospitable Bocay.

Wilfredo rarely left his post, but after the announcement of a particularly worrisome Central American diplomatic breakthrough, he came to Yamales to find out what was going on. I was spending a few days in the valley to measure ERN reaction to the diplomatic developments. ("So, Comandante, how do you feel about being screwed over by the Central American democracies?") I ran into Wilfredo in the headquarters area and asked him to stop by my tent after dinner.

He brought along a younger contra whom he introduced as his cousin. The resistance was riddled with family ties; in many cases these ties were an important bulwark for the cause—people carried on out of dedication to the memory of fallen brothers, or for brothers who fought on inside Nicaragua. I broke out the American cigarettes and made some coffee as we began a long discussion of the war and the future.

Wilfredo's story was fairly typical. He was from a poor, rural family; they had a farm and had developed a small trucking business. Originally hopeful about the Sandinistas, the family had grown disillusioned when they became aware of the practical implications of Sandinismo. Collectivized agriculture, government takeover (and elimination) of the free market for agricultural products, efforts to indoctrinate the children and put surveillance on potentially disloyal adults—the predictable manifestations of Communism went strongly against the grain of the fiercely independent and conservative Nicaraguan campesinos. I had heard the same story many times before in interviews with contras of all ranks. These people had joined the resistance because they could not accept life under Communism.

I have heard American academics speak condescendingly about the lack of political sophistication of peasants. "Unsophisticated" country people in the Third World, they say, don't really care if they live under a Communist or a non-Communist system; they are too unsophisticated to understand the difference. My conversations with Wilfredo and with scores of rural Nicaraguans just like him blasted big holes in this patronizing myth.

While Wilfredo and his brothers in arms could not engage in a debate on Engels, the dialectic, or historical materialism, they certainly understood and could speak passionately about the practical implications of Marxist Leninism. Time and time again I heard people who had formerly been farmers complain bitterly about the issues at the heart of the Communist program. People who knew nothing of Adam Smith decried (in simple campesino language) the manner in which the Sandinistas had tried to eliminate the market system that had determined prices in pre-Sandinista Nicaragua. The Sandinistas had ordered campesinos accustomed to working their own small plots to form "collective work brigades" that invariably failed to function as well as the old system of private land ownership. As consumers, the campesinos were no longer free to use their money as they saw fit. A ration system had replaced the free market.

Many visiting Americans clung to their cozy notions of indifferent campesinos incapable of understanding the difference between Communism and freedom. Upon hearing the complaints of the contras, they would often later rationalize that, "The contras aren't really interested in democracy; all they care about is their little economic problems." I didn't see it that way. Economics was at the heart of Marxist Leninism. Without the benefit of advanced degrees or analyses from the *New York Times Sunday Magazine*, the contras had been able to understand the essence of Communism. And they had violently rejected it.

I found it terribly ironic that the apparent worldwide decline of the Communist belief system should have such devastating consequences for the simple campesinos who had been driven to war precisely by their rejection of that system. Paradoxically, the contras would have been far better off with Josef Stalin in the Kremlin rather than Mikhail Gorbachev. That would have made it easier for them to get the U.S. help they needed. I suppose that such ironies would have been easier to accept had I been in Washington, but on the ground in Yamales, face-to-face with Wilfredo and his brothers in arms, it was hard to take. I admit to occasionally losing my battle for emotional detachment and objectivity. I sometimes lost sleep over the fate of the contras.

As cigarette smoke filled the tent, Wilfredo spoke of the horrors of the war. His voice cracked with emotion as he told of the long, hungry, dangerous marches into the Nicaraguan interior. The cousin sat silently and looked at the floor as Wilfredo spoke of the sacrifice of nine years of conflict, of the friends who had died in agony after being wounded deep inside Nicaragua. Talking to men like Wilfredo helped me to accomplish my mission in the valley—helped me to keep my finger on the pulse of the resistance. Talking to people like Wilfredo gave me a sense of the depth of the commitment to the struggle that existed among the Nicaraguan campesinos who formed the rank and file of the resistance. Most of the contras had made enormous investments in the war—investments in blood that they could not easily walk away from. Washington policymakers could be glib about the need to discard the "failed policy" that had support for the contras as its centerpiece, but the contras could not be so casual.

I asked Wilfredo what he thought would happen to the resistance. Many contras were fraudulently optimistic on this question and would tell me what they thought I wanted to hear. Others engaged in brave hyperbole. But Wilfredo was different, and I think he answered me truthfully: "I really don't know. I worry sometimes. Maybe this will all be decided in some air-conditioned office somewhere." It was a very nervous time for the Nicaraguan democratic resistance.

True Guerrillas

The more I worked with resistance members, the more willing I became to disregard the conventional wisdom about them. One of the first truisms I discarded had to do with the resistance's fighting prowess. After the $100 million U.S. lethal assistance program was approved, Gary Trudeau, author of the *Doonesbury* comic strip, got a lot of mileage out of the image of the contras as reluctant, craven, armchair warriors. "Comandante Less-Than-Zero" refused to leave his poolside command post in the "Big Goose" (Tegucigalpa) and falsified battle reports to satisfy his feckless American masters.

My experiences with the FMLN in El Salvador had left me somewhat susceptible to this line of criticism. I came away from El Salvador and Fort Bragg with a fairly good ability to evaluate guerrilla movements, and my initial impressions of the contras were not very favorable. One popular criticism posed this rhetorical question: "If six thousand FMLN guerrillas in El Salvador can seriously threaten the government there, why can't twelve thousand contras do the same to the Sandinistas?" It was a very good question. But the answer was complicated, and blame for the failure couldn't legitimately or fairly be placed on the contra combatants.

With the invidious comparisons between the contras and the FMLN in mind, when I first started working with the resistance I was on the lookout for true guerrillas. Surprisingly (in light of the rampant criticism of the supposedly incompetent contras), it didn't take me long to find them.

August 1988 brought a big exodus of resistance troops and civilian supporters from Nicaragua. Air drops to units inside Nicaragua had ended, and many contra units were finding it difficult to continue operations there. This fact in itself increased my suspicions about the guerrilla nature of the resistance: guerrillas shouldn't have been so dependent on outside assistance. But ironically, it was among those arriving in Honduras that August that I found my first promising evidence of real guerrillas in the resistance ranks.

"CH-5" was an officer in one of the Salazar regional commands. I met him at the Banco Grande infiltration point on the Coco River. Unlike later visits to Banco Grande, on this trip I found the place filled to capacity with contras and their supporters. They were coming out of Nicaragua. At first glance it looked like a rout, but I soon found out that the situation was not as bad as it looked.

Banco Grande was a great place to meet interesting people, and CH-5 was one of the most interesting. A thin, wiry man with long, almost shoulder-length hair, CH-5 had a very intense but calm look. He and his troops had come out of Nicaragua the previous day. He explained that most of the people at Banco Grande that day were not really full-fledged contras; most were new recruits who had rallied to resistance units in the Chontales-Boaco area deep inside Nicaragua. During the previous year, more and more new recruits had come to the ERN units, but without aerial resupply it had become very difficult to obtain arms for all of them. Resource shortages made training the recruits inside Nicaragua difficult, so CH-5 had been given the task of taking the large group to Honduras for training.

After asking CH-5 some questions about the difficult forty-day march from Chontales, I started to ask about life inside Nicaragua. How did they get food and ammunition? I also asked him how he viewed the war—how he thought the ERN could win it. I was shocked to find myself talking with someone who sounded like a real guerrilla fighter. CH-5's answers would have received high marks at Fort Bragg's guerrilla warfare school. Some sounded like they were straight from the pages of Mao Tse-tung or Che Guevara or Sun Tzu.

"Where do you get your food?"

"We get our food from supporters in the civilian population."

"Ammunition?"

"We get our ammunition from the Sandinistas."

"Is it difficult to get ammunition from the Sandinistas?"

(*Modestly*): "No, not really . . . all you have to do is kill them." (*Ghoulish giggles from the troops who were gathered around us*)

Later, my recounting of this response brought stunned silence to an embassy staff meeting when the ambassador interrupted talk of administrative issues and asked me to tell the group about my riverside chat with CH-5.

CH-5's troops were dressed in a strange mix of military clothing; many wore pieces of Sandinista uniforms. He pulled the banana-shaped magazine from his AK-47 rifle and told me to examine the cartridges: "Half from you, half from the *Piricuacos*!" He explained that the shiny brass cartridges had been captured from the Sandinistas; those with a darker tint on the brass were leftovers from the $100 million U.S. lethal assistance program. *Piricuaco* ("Piri" for short) was the contras' slang term for the Sandinistas; it means "rabid dog."

At Fort Bragg I had been taught that the source of supply is one of the factors that distinguish true guerrillas from conventional soldiers. Conventional soldiers depend on supply lines from the rear. Guerrillas receive their sustenance from civilian supporters; their munitions are either homemade or procured from the enemy. As CH-5's Sandinista-clothed and -armed troops gathered around in the makeshift tent in which we talked, I began to suspect that I had discovered some genuine guerrillas.

CH-5 had all of the appropriate guerrilla warfare lines: "We are not the owners of this struggle. The people are the owners of the struggle. We are just their advance guard!" He could have been telling me what he thought I wanted to hear, of course, but the fact that CH-5 had successfully fought for six months inside Nicaragua after the cutoff of U.S. lethal aid was sufficient reason to take him seriously. Throughout our conversation, CH-5 exhibited a solid understanding of the central importance of popular support in guerrilla warfare. He pointed out that his unit could have continued operations indefinitely—indeed, most of his unit remained in their operating area—and he was openly scornful of ERN units that had been unable to continue the fight without U.S. lethal assistance. "Those guys had let themselves become airdrop–dependent! We learned to use to the maximum everything available to us." Defective mortar rounds, for example, were rigged to serve as improvised boobytraps.

CH-5's scorn for his airdrop–dependent colleagues was right on the mark. Some ERN officers refused to consider the guerrilla option. I had heard that the subject of guerrilla supply systems had come up in earlier discussions of how the contras should respond to the halting of U.S. air drops, and somebody had mentioned the Ho Chi Minh Trail. One of the non-guerrilla commanders had strongly rejected the idea, shouting, "No somos chinos!" (We're not Chinese!)

When I asked CH-5 what needed to be done for the ERN to win the war, he gave me the answer of a guerrilla—the answer of someone who understands the decisive role of popular support in guerrilla warfare. Instead of talking about the ridiculous prospect of ERN units slugging it out with the Sandinistas and marching on Managua, CH-5 spoke of a massive political action effort to build support in the urban areas. This campaign would be complemented by ERN civic action and propaganda efforts designed to consolidate support in the countryside.

I returned to Tegucigalpa excited by my discovery of real guerrilla warriors in the ERN and spent most of that weekend drafting my report. In dozens of subsequent interviews with members of the ERN, I encountered people who, like CH-5, understood and practiced the principles of guerrilla warfare. Unfortunately, I also discovered that the strategic politico-military leadership that should have complemented this kind of expertise simply did not exist.

Comandante Less-Than-Zero

The contras undeniably had severe problems, but I think that many people failed to understand the true nature of those shortcomings. Distant critics regularly blasted the contras for their lack of success on the battlefield, and it became somewhat axiomatic that the contras had bad leadership. For many Americans, *Doonesbury*'s Comandante Less-Than-Zero became the image of a contra commander. Although the resistance leadership was far from perfect, I think that most of the criticism I heard from outsiders was misplaced and unfair.

I found that there were many levels of resistance leadership. Unfortunately, the degree of dedication and competence the leaders exhibited had an inverse relationship to their distance from the battlefield, while the level of public exposure and selfishness was directly proportional to this distance. It seemed to me that the closer you got to the actual battlefield (Banco Grande was as close as I could get), the more likely you were to find dedicated, selfless patriots like Wilfredo and CH-5—people who understood the principles of guerrilla warfare and were putting their lives on the line for their country. Conversely, the greater the distance from the battlefield, the more likely you were to find Comandantes Less-Than-Zero. The leadership problem was not on the battlefield; it was at the critical strategic level—the level that should have provided the ERN with long-range vision, political guidance, and international representation. While heroic Nicaraguan campesinos struggled and suffered in the field, they were led and represented at the strategic level by an ineffective Political Directorate that contributed absolutely no strategic leadership and grossly misrepresented the contras to the world.

During my time in Honduras I continued a study of Communist insurgencies that I had begun in preparation for my mission in El Salvador. I read about the FMLN and the Viet Cong. This was a depressing activity for somebody working with the resistance, because the contrasts between the Communist guerrilla forces and the contras were striking.

The contrasts were not at the troop or combat commander level. The field units showed real devotion to the cause. On many occasions when I reached out to shake the hand of a resistance member, the hand that met mine was mangled or missing fingers as a result of war wounds. The contras had been at war for a very long time.

Likewise, I found the regional commanders (battalion commanders) to be a very impressive group of young leaders. During my time in the valley, the General Staff grew into an effective and dedicated senior leadership team. Of course, even at this level things were often disorganized and chaotic, but I reminded myself that this was a completely come-as-you-are, nonprofessional army made up of peasant volunteers—it couldn't be expected to run at a high level of efficiency. The really disturbing contrasts were at higher levels.

The contras simply did not have the kind of political leadership that gave Communist guerrilla movements such cohesion and direction. Descriptions of the FMLN or the Viet Cong refer constantly to the party and the political cadres. This political leadership is the heart, soul, and brain of successful guerrilla movements. Not only does it provide political cohesion and direction, in a successful guerrilla movement it also provides strategic military direction. Because the military actions mounted by a guerrilla movement are carried out for their political and psychological impact, the quality of the strategic political leadership is of obvious importance.

One night in Yamales, I went to the improvised shack that served as the living quarters of the ERN's new military leader: Israel Galeano, a.k.a. Comandante Franklyn. Franklyn had a long and distinguished record in the ERN; that was why the Council of Commanders had chosen him as their new senior commander. He was of humble campesino origins, and in this sense was in a good position to lead and represent the peasant army. But at the same time, his background had not afforded him the kind of educational opportunities available to someone like Miguel Castellanos.

At first glance Franklyn did not give the impression of being a contemplative person. He was a big, somewhat heavyset fellow. His mustache, his cowboy hat, his swagger, and the cigarette that drooped from his lips all conjured up images of the stereotypical Mexican bad guy of low-budget westerns. He always seemed to have several weapons strapped to various parts of his body—multiple knives and pistols at the ready. One afternoon, as I was walking through the Strategic Command Headquarters area, I was startled by a very loud explosion. I turned and found Franklyn standing in a cloud of gun smoke. He had acquired a new chrome-plated .357 Magnum and apparently wanted to see how much damage it would do to a nearby tree. On the surface, Franklyn just didn't seem like a philosophical kind of guy. But appearances can be deceiving.

That night in Yamales I found Franklyn seated at a homemade desk. He was listening to a shortwave radio broadcast of international news and reading from a collection of books on military history—the kind of cheap books sold at supermarket checkout counters or on late-night TV commercials. ("For a limited time only, you can have this twenty-volume set on the greatest military leaders of all time for the low, low price of $19.99.") Franklyn was obviously feeling the weight of his new responsibilities and was trying to educate himself for the tasks ahead.

He told me that he had been reading about Douglas MacArthur. We sat and talked for a while about MacArthur and war and the resistance and the future. I admired Franklyn's dedication and his effort to prepare himself, but I left the shack feeling a little ashamed. Here I was, a representative of the world's leading democracy, working with people trying to overthrow a tyranny, and their leaders were trying to figure out how to do it by reading supermarket military history. I left that meeting with Franklyn feeling that we had seriously let these poor people down.

The resistance's Political Directorate was supposed to provide the contras with the kind of strategic guidance and leadership that Communist guerrillas got from the Communist Party, but the Directorate was a hopelessly distant and ineffective organization. It was composed of seven men, each representing a different faction of the Nicaraguan opposition. Unfortunately, the Directorate was based in Miami and had little contact with the combatants. Watching the interplay between the ERN and the Directorate, I began to understand why the Salvadoran FMLN had insisted that their politicos—like Miguel Castellanos—have at least a smattering of military experience: it gave them credibility among the troops and the ability to understand their problems. Unfortunately, I saw no such credibility or understanding in the relationship between the resistance's Political Directorate and the ERN combatants.

My contacts were with the military members of the ERN, and my view of the Directorate is colored by their views. The contras in the field viewed the directors—with the exception of Enrique Bermudez and to some extent Aristedes Sanchez—as distant, self-centered, scheming politicians who were making a living off the resistance. The troops lived in the field; the directors lived in Miami. The troops were mostly dark-skinned campesinos; the directors (with the exception of Wycliffe Diego) were mostly light-skinned, educated city people. Except for Bermudez, the directors rarely (if ever) visited Yamales. In my year with the resistance, Adolfo Calero came to Yamales exactly once (he did not stay the night). Alfredo César never appeared. Montalvan, Ferrey, and Sanchez made one or two guest appearances. Wycliffe Diego, the Indian representative, couldn't speak Spanish very well and didn't visit.

I was once slightly embarrassed at an embassy reception when the ambassador introduced me to a group of visiting U.S. congressmen as "one of our experts on the resistance." The embarrassment came when one of the congressmen asked me about the Directorate. I was at a loss to provide much information. In fact, I momentarily forgot how many directors there were. The congressman must have wondered about the level of our expertise, but the next day, in front of a formation of some seven thousand contra combatants, I pulled the congressman aside and told him that I really didn't pay much attention to the Directorate. I pointed to the crowd and told him that these were the people I worked with. The congressman got the point: the Nicaraguan resistance was an army of campesinos in the field, not a group of politicians in Miami.

Wrapped up in egocentric, internecine squabbles in far-off Florida, the Directorate was obviously in no position to provide the politico-military leadership the troops needed to wage a successful guerrilla war. In time, I came to view the problem as a corollary of the "decapitation" problem I had observed in El Salvador: our team lacked the educated intellectuals needed to wage the political-ideological portion of the war. For the Nicaraguan elite it was *Patria libre o Miami!* ("Give me a free country or I'll go to Miami!"—a sarcastic variation of *Patria libre o muerte!* "free country or death.") The well-educated Nicaraguans who could have formed the resistance's democratic equivalent of the Communist Party decamped not to austere Yamales, but to the comfort of San Jose or Miami. There were some exceptions. The resistance's very dedicated medical doctors lived in Yamales, but for the most part the Nicaraguan elite had done exactly what their Salvadoran counterparts had done: they had fled to Miami and left the campesinos to fight the war. Poor Franklyn was left in Yamales trying to learn about strategic leadership from supermarket history books.

The Miami-based Directorate did additional damage to the cause by presenting to the world a grotesquely distorted image of the resistance. My encounter with the congressman is a good example of this. At the ambassador's residence, he was asking me about the resistance and thinking of the Miami Directorate. When I thought of the resistance, I thought of the field commanders and the troops. This was an important and telling disconnect. The campesino combatants were very poorly served by the politicians who "represented" them in Washington and Miami.

Someone told me that a U.S. senator had described the contras as "those shits." I was disturbed and angered by the remark until I realized that the senator had to be referring to the Miami Directorate. This was another example of a phenomenon I had observed with congressmen. When Washington observers thought of the contras, the image that probably came to mind was

Comandante Less-Than-Zero and his Miami *comandos* lounging at poolside. What a tragedy.

The U.S. government contributed to this leadership disaster. Washington officials seemed to like having the Directorate nearby in Miami. They liked to be able to zip down to Florida and then go back to Washington to tell their bosses that they had been "down talking to the contras." I was always amused when Washington-based officers spoke of the people in Miami as the "resistance." We in the embassy had picked up the Yamales habit of referring to those people as the "Directorate" or "the Miami Directorate." For us, "the resistance" meant the campesino army in the field.

Language played an important role in exacerbating misunderstandings about the contras. We Americans have an unfortunate tendency to equate English-language skills with intelligence. Those who lack such skills are considered either deficient in intelligence or poorly educated. Likewise, Americans rarely bother to become proficient in a foreign language. The Washington players on our side who didn't speak Spanish inevitably focused their attention on those Nicaraguans who spoke English (almost always the Miami-based directors and their acolytes). In Yamales, I once watched a Washington-based, non-Spanish-speaking State Department official wander uncomfortably among the military leaders of the contras—unable to communicate—until he spotted a visiting Directorate politico from Miami who spoke English. The visiting gringo spent most of his time yakking with his English-speaking pal and then doubtless returned to Washington to report authoritatively on "contra attitudes." He could have saved the taxpayers a lot of money by just going to Miami. I remember thinking that this was the way we selected the first Somoza: he spoke good English.

I have heard a lot of excuses for the Directorate's failure to supply the leadership the contras needed, and some of them are valid. A democratically oriented group like the resistance is inherently more difficult to lead than an ideologically monolithic organization like the FMLN or the Sandinistas. The factious, fractious nature of Nicaraguan politics made political direction even more difficult (as they told me, they can be stubborn *mucos*), but it is the Nicaraguans themselves who bear the ultimate responsibility for their inability to get together.

Some would place all the blame for this lack of political direction on the United States. I think that we have to accept part of the responsibility, but only a small part of it. Over the history of the movement, I think our efforts to shape the political leadership of the contras were fairly inept. Although I wasn't involved with the resistance at the time, I have the impression that the Directorate was formed more as a public relations trick to win support on Capitol Hill than as an effort to provide real strategic leadership for the resistance movement.

One of the reasons why we failed to help provide the contras with effective politico-military leadership was because we ourselves never really understood the need for it. Very few people in the U.S. government have any understanding of guerrilla warfare—how it is fought and how it is won. Many of the U.S. officials who visited Honduras during my time there seemed to be hoping for a renewal of lethal aid not so the resistance could wage a guerrilla campaign—instead these officers had what seemed to me a thoroughly unrealistic notion about some sort of conventional march on Managua. Many in Congress seemed to have similar ideas; the contras were often pilloried on the Hill for their "failure to hold territory." I wonder how many poor young contras died trying to jump through the hoops that these dilettantes held up for them.

One of the Reagan administration's biggest mistakes was failing to explain the goals of its Central America policy to the American people. Instead of an honest and straightforward explanation, the public was fed a series of rationalizations: first we were supporting the contras only so they could "interdict arms" en route to El Salvador; then we were supporting them in order to force the Sandinistas to negotiate, and then to force elections. Often, government officials simply "refused to comment on covert operations."

I think that the interest of the United States would have been much better served by an early, straightforward announcement of our intent to help the Nicaraguan resistance in their efforts to overthrow the Marxist-Leninist Sandinista regime. Former assistant secretary of state Elliott Abrams seems to have reached a similar conclusion. In an April 4, 1988, interview with the *New York Times*, Abrams commented that "the administration should have taken this question to the American people very soon after the inauguration, should have stated that this was a major national security problem, should have launched a large campaign to use the President's popularity to get the people behind open and significant actions to counter the Communist threat that was coming from Nicaragua."

One reason for our failure to announce our objectives may have been the attitude of some of the neighboring Central American governments. Some of them preferred to pretend that the contras either did not exist or were all in Nicaragua. Many in the region opposed the contras because of a knee-jerk opposition to anything that smacked of U.S. intervention. But the Nicaraguan resistance was really an indigenous movement. We were helping the resistance, but it was not—as many critics allege—a creation of the U.S. government. Nicaraguans had risen up against the Sandinistas long before Uncle Sam arrived on the scene, and they continued to fight long after we delivered our last item of lethal assistance.

As for the morality of supporting a group that was working to overthrow a government, I think it is important to remember that as Marxist Leninists, the Sandinistas themselves openly advocated the violent overthrow of our system of government and very actively supported efforts to overthrow neighboring governments.

Years after I left the Yamales, David McCullough's book *1776* seemed to carry me back to contra valley. McCullough's description of Washington's ragtag, unprofessional, regionally organized, come-as-you-are force of poor farmers motivated by economic injustice reminded me a lot of the contras. The improvised housing used by Washington's army during the siege of Boston ("Tents and shelters were mainly patched-together concoctions of whatever could be found") was strikingly reminiscent of the improvised shacks of Comandante Franklyn and his troops. The embattled farmers of the contra regional commands had a lot in common with those of the New England militias. It is a shame that more people didn't see these similarities.

Americans who argue that the Nicaraguan people were wrong to rise up against the Sandinistas should go back and reread our Declaration of Independence. And American critics who argued against the propriety of U.S. support for insurgent groups seemed to ignore the foreign assistance that we received during our revolution. As I watched the spectacle that we all perpetrated in Yamales in 1988 and 1989, I often felt like climbing one of the peaks and, thinking of that young French officer who had helped George Washington, shouting in exasperation, "Lafayette, we have forgotten!"

Sometimes I felt that the individual contra troopers were the only noble players in the whole sad game. Abandoned by the Nicaraguan elite, let down and misrepresented by their own political leadership, whipsawed by on-again, off-again support from a vacillating U.S. government, and shunned by their Central American brothers, the poor Nicaraguan campesino army hung in there month after month in the Yamales Valley.

CHAPTER 8
THE MISKITO COAST
MISSILE CRISIS

Now I'm hiding in Honduras
I'm a desperate man . . .
Send lawyers, guns, and money . . .
The shit has hit the fan!

> —From the song "Lawyers, Guns and Money"
> by Warren Zevon, 1981

BLASS WAS SUPPOSED TO MEET ME AT THE AIRPORT. I was a little annoyed by his absence, but it didn't surprise me. Plans change on the Miskito Coast, and communication with the outside world is often impossible. It is a place where you have to roll with the punches. As I climbed out of the Twin Otter airplane that had carried me from La Ceiba, I surveyed the desolate savanna that surrounds Puerto Lempira and wondered how I was going to make contact with the contra Indians I had come to visit.

Puerto Lempira ("PL" to the cognoscenti) is the largest town in the Honduran Mosquitia—the Honduran portion of the famed Miskito Coast. On my previous visits the region had fully lived up to its colorful, exotic, and wild reputation. *Newsweek* had dubbed the zone "the Wild, Wild East," and indeed it was a land of cowboys and Indians, pirates, and smugglers. With my backpack, blue jeans, jungle boots, Ray-Bans, and New York Yankees baseball cap, I must have looked like a modern-day cowboy. And I had, in fact, come to see the Indians. Blass was their leader.

In late 1988 no roads connected Puerto Lempira with the rest of Honduras—if you wanted to go there, you had to fly in or go by boat. I had used the little commercial airline that services the north coast of Honduras. The roundabout route that I took from Tegucigalpa to Puerto Lempira accentuated the region's isolation. Departing Tegucigalpa on a commercial Boeing 707, I had landed in the coastal city of La Ceiba, Honduras. Facing an eight-hour layover, I had decided to go out to the island of Roatán for a little tourism while waiting for the flight into the Mosquitia. The side trip to Roatán provided reminders of how far from home I really was.

Roatán is a scuba-diving paradise that caters to Americans who jet in to swim among the coral and the tropical fish. I suppose my blue jeans and jungle boots made me look like a confusing mix of traveling graduate student and mercenary. Indeed, the tourists seemed confused by my presence among them. Most of them were young couples who only hours or days earlier had been back in their homes in suburban America. As we tooled around the little islands in the resort's taxi boat, they eyed me with suspicion and plied me with cautious questions: "Sylvia and I just flew in from Kennedy. Uh . . . where are *you* from?" The afternoon passed, and soon I was back on the plane bound for the Mosquitia, en route to another planet.

While I am sure that my arrival in Puerto Lempira must have raised suspicions, there was nothing covert or secretive about my trip: I was an embassy officer on a completely overt reporting mission. But Blass's absence put me in an awkward position. I thought he might have sent a representative, but there was nobody standing there with a sign saying CONTRAS or BILL MEARA—AMERICAN EMBASSY. I looked through the crowd and tried to spot somebody who might have been sent to meet me. (Thank God there was no airport terminal public address system; the possible announcements were frightening: "Will the representative of the Nicaraguan democratic resistance please meet his embassy contact at the information desk.")

I must have scared the daylights out of a couple of young fellows when I walked up and, as discretely as possible, asked if they were from YATAMA. They shook their heads and backed away very quickly. Before things could turn from the comic to the ridiculous, I slung my backpack over my shoulder and walked into PL. The adventure was about to begin.

Puerto Lempira is, in my somewhat unconventional opinion, a charming little town. Unlike most of Honduras, it has a distinctly Caribbean flavor. Sandwiched between the airstrip and Caratasca Bay, its colorful buildings are mostly older wooden structures; many are built on stilts. I was on my way to a refugee office to inquire about Blass's whereabouts when the guerrilla commander burst out of the local Honduran army outpost and embraced me like a long-lost brother.

Blass was a thirty-three-year-old Miskito Indian. He had grown up on the banks of the Coco, the river that forms the border between Honduras and Nicaragua. Before the war he had managed to spend a few years in college; he was a thoughtful and philosophical person. After years of combat inside Nicaragua, he had been pressed into service as the top leader of YATAMA. In time, I came to realize that Blass was more than just a guerrilla commander — he was an important tribal leader of the Miskito people. He worried about the future of the refugees and the old people and the little Miskito kids.

The Miskitos are a fascinating bunch. Mosquitia, their homeland, extends in an arc from the central portion of the northern coast of Honduras across the mouth of the Coco River down and along the Atlantic coast of Nicaragua. There are about 250,000 Miskitos. I found them to be very gentle people. They speak their own language; I tried to learn a few words — they taught me to say "hello," "good-bye," "have a nice day," "water," and "woman." They were very fond of Americans and loved it when we showed an interest in their history and culture.

I'm not sure why, but SLO's relations with YATAMA always seemed a little easier than our interactions with the ERN-N. Perhaps the Indians were closer to us culturally (they had been influenced by British pirates who worked along the Caribbean coast), or maybe it was just that we didn't interact enough with YATAMA to get on each other's nerves. The Indians also retained an element of the novel and exotic. In any case, Blass and his Indian warriors apparently really liked the Americans sent to work with them. They eventually gave some of us Indian "war names" and even issued us YATAMA identification cards. So, yes, I was a card-carrying contra. I am Comandante Tahplu, "the bad-tempered warrior," and I have the YATAMA ID card to prove it.

Whenever I spoke to Blass and the Miskitos, I had to remind myself that I was dealing with people who had exotic beliefs and customs — including witch doctors and potions and spells. Although some people look down on the customs of indigenous people, I found it useful in such situations to recall some of the rituals of my own Catholic upbringing, like holy water and incense.

On the day I arrived, Blass was managing the latest episode in the never-end-ing crisis that characterized YATAMA's relations with the local Honduran army battalion. Apologizing for his failure to meet me at the airport, Blass explained that twenty-six members of his staff had been arrested by the Honduran army. He himself had apparently been spared that indignity because of a recent "lay-ing on of hands" by the U.S. ambassador. The ambassador had flown out to visit Blass after a particularly nasty incident in which Honduran soldiers had staked Blass down in a pit filled neck-high with mud. Blass had been forced to stand on the tips of his toes to keep his nose and mouth out of the mud.

I learned that the Hondurans were now charging Blass's men with a crime that seemed entirely consistent with the Mosquitia's wild ambiance: piracy. Apparently some Honduran fishermen had been robbed at gunpoint by per-sons reported to be members of YATAMA. I had no way of knowing whether Blass's men were guilty or innocent, but the Mosquitia was definitely the kind of place where people still committed piracy. The mundane crimes of twentieth-century civilization—tax evasion, insider trading—were not on the docket in Puerto Lempira.

Blass was very glad to see me, probably because he was not sure how long the ambassador's benediction would keep him out of jail; as we walked through town he stood very close to me to make sure everyone knew that the gringo from the embassy had come specifically to see him. He told me that we had to go to the local army outpost to check on the status of his jailed troops.

I was not going to interfere with Honduran justice in any way, but I thought it wouldn't hurt if the Hondurans knew that the American embassy was closely following events in the Mosquitia. Blass and I walked into the little shack that served as the Honduran battalion's local headquarters. I was pleased to see that the captain on duty was very concerned about my presence. His questions about my identity, itinerary, and job responsibilities bordered on an interrogation. I answered all of his questions; his eyes widened when I told him that I was a special assistant to the U.S. ambassador and that I had come out to visit "our friend Blass." I even gave him my business card.

The captain couldn't tell us much (predictably, he was awaiting word from a superior officer), so Blass and I set out on a motorcycle for YATAMA's secret hideout to see the few staffers who had managed to evade capture. I soon found myself sharing a basement refuge with five very worried Miskito guerrillas. On a little radio in the corner, Blass communicated in the Miskito language with units deployed in the field while his companions kept a lookout for Honduran soldiers.

After much consultation, Blass concluded that there was nothing to do but wait for the Hondurans to make the next move. Blass was particularly worried that the Honduran battalion would not return the munitions and supplies they had confiscated from the prisoners; since the February 1988 cutoff of U.S. military assistance, supplies had become very scarce.

With nothing to do but wait, it was decided that I would return to my boardinghouse in town. I invited Blass and his girlfriend (one of the best-looking girls in all of the Mosquitia) to dinner, and we agreed to meet at eight. I told Blass to bring along anyone else he might want to invite. On a borrowed motorcycle I roared out of the hideout and onto the savanna of the Mosquitia. The sun was setting as I took a little cross-country detour on my way back to town. I couldn't resist the urge to open that motorcycle up and make a little noise. I remember thinking how lucky I was — I was actually getting paid for this. But I felt a little sad, too, because I knew that my diplomatic career would never again offer opportunities for adventures like this.

I was staying at the boardinghouse of Doña Maria, a woman large in both physique and spirit. Doña Maria was Puerto Lempira's entrepreneur. She was the local travel agent, and she ran a number of other businesses out of her bayside facility. The food and the ambiance at Doña Maria's were always excellent.

Dinner that night typified the bizarre nature of the contra war in the Mosquitia. Totally in keeping with the area's surreal atmosphere, Blass and his lady showed up for dinner in the company of the Honduran army sergeant who was the jailer of his troops. This was Blass's invited guest. I couldn't believe it. When I pulled Blass aside, he shrugged and explained, "Well, he's not really a bad guy, and besides, I want to stay on his good side."

We had a very pleasant dinner at Doña Maria's. The sergeant was courteous and well behaved. After dinner he excused himself, saying that he had to attend to his duties. Blass, his girlfriend, and I took our drinks out onto the dock and watched the moonlight shimmering on the water as Blass talked about the war. He was close to despair. I tried to cheer him up, but there was not much that I could say. We finished our drinks and said goodnight.

A few hours later, at one o'clock in the morning, the sergeant with whom we had so cordially dined went to the girlfriend's house (where Blass was staying) and confiscated Blass's pickup truck. He apparently needed to go somewhere and had decided to take advantage of a Miskito, dinner diplomacy notwithstanding. Blass had a hard life in the Mosquitia twilight zone.

The following morning, we returned to the battalion outpost for an update on the status of the imprisoned troops. Nobody in authority was present, so Blass and I sat down on the front steps to wait for the sergeant or the captain to arrive. One young Honduran sentry patrolled the front porch; he carried a rifle that was almost as big as he was and wore a too-big helmet that wobbled on his head.

Blass was clearly tired of all the "Honduran bullshit." I got the impression that he would have much preferred to be back inside Nicaragua fighting Sandinistas. Nervous and edgy, he got up to pace around on the porch. After a couple of minutes he returned to my side, grabbed my arm, looked me dead in the eye, and said very quietly, "They have a missile!"

We had given the Nicaraguan resistance shoulder-fired Redeye missiles, which they used to shoot down Sandinista helicopters. The Honduran armed forces didn't have such weapons and were jealous of the contras' surface-to-air capability. With an eye on the sentry I asked for details. Just like a scene from a movie, we feigned chitchat as we quietly discussed where the missile was located and what we should do about it.

Blass explained that the missile was in this very building, in a little office that had an entrance from the porch. I was determined to get a look for myself. I couldn't return to the embassy and say that "I think" the Hondurans "might" have a surface-to-air missile. Doing my best to ascertain some pattern in the sentry's aimless ramblings, I waited until he seemed to be farthest from the office entrance and had his back toward me. I got up as if to stretch, ambled over to the entrance . . . and decided to go for it. Placing my hands on the door frame, I quickly stuck my head into the office and looked down. Sure enough, on the floor of the office was a big, ugly, olive drab container labeled ROCKET PROJECTILE WITH EXPLOSIVE WARHEAD. It was definitely a Redeye antiaircraft surface-to-air missile. The Hondurans had apparently taken it from a platoon of YATAMA troops who had been deployed near the mouth of the Coco River.

Anticipating the questions, denials, and investigations certain to ensue, I took note of the missile's serial number. I am bad with numbers, so I kept repeating it in my head until I finally had a chance to write it down (on my hand). Now I had to get the information to the embassy. Blass's situation seemed to have stabilized, and I felt that I had sufficiently demonstrated U.S. interest in his health and welfare. There were no telephone lines out of Puerto Lempira, and the telegraph system was out of service. The only communication with the outside world was through shortwave radios operated by missionaries, and I certainly wasn't going to broadcast this news over shortwave radio. I had to fly out of the Mosquitia and find a phone booth. Blass drove me to the airport on his motorcycle. As I was leaving I learned that the imprisoned YATAMA troops were about to be released.

I flew to La Ceiba and called the embassy to report the essential facts, then went to a restaurant where I had lunch and drafted my reporting cable. Later that afternoon I flew back to Tegucigalpa. While the Hondurans at first denied having the missile, because we were able to say that a U.S. officer had seen it and had noted the serial number, we were eventually able to get it back.

Because the Mosquitia was so difficult to get to, and because the Northern Front was so much bigger (ten times the size of YATAMA), our contact with Blass and his troops was relatively infrequent. To compensate, and because Blass was a likable fellow, we tried to have dinner with him whenever he came to Tegucigalpa. He had to come into town every month or so to argue with the bean counters from USAID. Knowing very well what a frustrating experience that could be, we always tried to cheer Blass up over dinner.

At first I had my housekeeper whip up some spaghetti or hamburgers—simple chow that I thought would appeal to our Indian guests. I quickly learned that the Miskitos were particular about their food. During one of our first dinners, Blass suddenly looked up from his plate and asked, "Where's the rice?" When I told him that we hadn't planned to serve rice, he sighed and said, "For us, if there is no rice, it is not considered a meal!" Miskitos can be very straightforward. After that we took him to restaurants. Tegucigalpa is not exactly the culinary capital of the Western world, but we found a couple of places that Blass liked. Since Miskitos like chicken and rice, we started to frequent the Chinese restaurants of Tegoose—where both items were always available.

Just before I was transferred from Honduras, Blass came to town and we arranged for one last dinner at a Chinese restaurant. On this trip he had brought along his five-year-old son. As we walked into the restaurant, I pondered the many incongruities of the scene: Blass was a warrior with many enemies. He was in real danger in Tegucigalpa—he was always in danger. But he was also a father who wanted to spend time with his son. We picked a table near a fish tank so the boy could look at the fish while his dad and I talked about the war and life and glasnost and the Sandinistas. As the little boy sat mesmerized by the fish, Blass told me about the night his son was born. The boy came into the world in a contra camp near the Coco River, and his first crib was made of empty ammunition cases and camouflage military blankets. Blass had ordered a mortar barrage to herald his son's birth.

The boy spoke to his father in Miskito. This was his first trip to a city. In the car on the way to the restaurant Blass had laughed as he translated his son's wide-eyed questions: "Who owns all these cars? Why are there so many lights?" Blass talked of his own childhood in the isolated Mosquitia and recalled being frightened the first time he saw an airplane.

Over dessert, Blass talked about the personal danger he lived with. He wasn't particularly afraid of dying, but he did worry about what would happen to his son. Months later, in Spain, I read of the death of a Miskito contra commander. It wasn't Blass . . . but it could have been.

CHAPTER 9
STAIRWAY TO HEAVEN

If our engine quits, we'll auto-rotate down to the tree-tops. We'll lose the rotor when we hit the top canopy. Then we'll fall a long way to the ground. We'll hit hard and we'll have little chance of surviving. It won't be pretty.

— A pilot during a gloomy moment over the endless Honduran triple-canopy foliage

MY TRIPS TO THE YAMALES VALLEY were almost always by helicopter. USAID had a contract with a New Orleans company called Air Logistics. Under the contract, "Air Log" based two pilots and two helicopters at Tegucigalpa's Toncontin Airport. Bruce English and Roger Thompson and their two very trustworthy Bell Jet Ranger helicopters became a lifeline for the contras. Almost every day, Roger and Bruce flew missions to keep the contras alive. Both of these superb pilots were survivors of the Vietnam War's most deadly helicopter campaigns. It was a pleasure and privilege to fly with them.

Air Log Honduras certainly had one of the world's most bizarre and dangerous flight schedules. In my efforts to keep in touch with the contras, I made weekly use of the Air Log flights. On a typical flight we would rendezvous at 7:00 a.m. at Toncontin. The pilots would have been given a vague set of instructions from the bureaucrats who were managing the aid program.

Sometimes we carried doctors out to the various field clinics. Other flights shuttled food to areas that couldn't be reached by supply trucks or parachute air drops.[1]

During the dry season the helicopter flights were a lot of fun. The mountainous Honduran countryside was spectacular. During one flight Roger brought along a second set of earphones for his Sony Walkman. Suspended in the deep blue sky, high above the rugged, bright green terrain, we played "Stairway to Heaven" and let the rock group Led Zeppelin carry us to the Yamales Strategic Command.

Flying east out of Toncontin Airport, the helicopters always passed over my house. On days when I wasn't engaged in contra liaison I could watch the Air Log choppers fly out to the border as I got dressed for another day in the embassy.

Flying was more difficult during the rainy season. Honduras is made up a series of mountain ranges that (somehow appropriately) follow no discernible pattern. (A Honduran diplomat at the UN was once asked to describe his country's terrain. He produced a piece of writing paper, crumbled it into a ball, and then pulled it open: "There," he said, "that's what it's like!") Clouds frequently obscured the peaks. Roger and Bruce flew strictly VFR (under visual flight rules)—they had no instruments that would allow them to "fly blind" through clouds. If we entered a cloud and lost sight of the ground, there was a distinct possibility of hitting a mountainside at high speed. So, during the rainy season the pilots had to engage in the tricky and dangerous business of "looking for a hole"—trying to find a spot where the clouds did not obscure the peaks of the particular mountain range we were trying to get past. Many times, Roger or Bruce had to spin the helicopter around when clouds suddenly plugged a promising hole.

There were other dangers besides the weather. "Bird strikes" were common. The closest we ever came to losing a helicopter was when Bruce English's Jet Ranger was struck in the windshield by a six-pound hawk. (I was in the embassy that day.) The bird blasted through the windshield and hit Bruce in the face, knocking him unconscious. A fixed-wing airplane will continue to fly or glide forward if left unattended, but a helicopter will begin to spin and flip and plummet to the earth. With Bruce unconscious and five passengers onboard (there was no co-pilot), that is just what happened. Long experience in the pilot's seat paid off that afternoon when Bruce—in spite of serious eye injuries—regained consciousness (at about three hundred feet) and was able to retake control of the chopper.

Sandinista missile strikes were a constant danger as well. Weather often required us to fly very close to the Nicaraguan border. It was always a little eerie to look out the side of the chopper and peer down the Jalapa Valley of Nicaragua. On a clear day you could see a long way into the country. The Sandinistas could have hit us with one of their shoulder-fired heat-seeking SAMs, so we took precautions when flying close to Nicaragua.

The pilots faced additional dangers in the landing zones near the border. During the summer of 1988, hundreds of contras were coming out of Nicaragua. Many of them were in very poor physical condition; some were suffering from severe malnutrition. We had to get food to them quickly, and that meant flying supplies right down to the border-crossing points on the Coco River. Because USAID officers rarely flew on these missions, Roger and Bruce (neither of whom was fluent in Spanish) were left with the difficult task of dealing with the hungry and heavily armed contras waiting in the landing zone (LZ). These encounters could be very dicey.

The pilots and I became quite adept at keeping the LZ chaos under control. Roger and Bruce operated under a very legalistic and unrealistic set of rules sent down from Washington. While engaged in supply missions they could legally carry sick or wounded contras to the hospital at Yamales on a space-available basis. The decision as to who qualified as sick or wounded was left to the pilots. There was to be absolutely no transportation of weaponry. The rule about the weapons sounded reasonable in the air-conditioned conference rooms at the embassy, but on the ground at Banco Grande it wasn't very practical. The helicopter would land, and before we could even get the doors open, the gaunt warriors would be mobbing the aircraft, placing their rifles and rucksacks in the aft cargo compartment. While the pilot tried to sort out the messy passenger manifest, I would try to locate officers. And at the same time both of us would be trying to keep the hungry and desperate Nicaraguans from walking around the back of the helo and into the tail rotor. All this took place under whirling rotors with time pressure imposed by the fact that we were wasting limited daylight and burning limited fuel.

One afternoon, Roger and I were accompanied by two USAID officials from Washington whose main purpose seemed to be contra tourism. They asked a lot of stupid questions. (Stupid question: "Why is he flying so low?" Scornful answer: "To avoid antiaircraft missiles!") On landing at the Banco Grande crossing point, we were met by a motley group of gaunt young contras and newly arrived refugees who had just completed a very harrowing escape from Nicaragua. We were the first Americans most of them had ever met. The combatants represented a number of different contra units, so it was difficult to find an officer who could exert authority over the entire bunch. It was hot and very humid. The helicopter's engine was roaring and emitting nauseating fumes, babies were screaming, and everybody there was trying to push into the five available helicopter seats. Having just walked for forty hungry days to get out of Nicaragua, the new arrivals were understandably eager to avoid an additional four-day march to the Yamales Valley.

During my year with the contras, I never once felt that I was in any danger from them. A Sandinista infiltrator might have decided to do away with a visiting American, but the presence of thousands of heavily armed pro-American contras made such a project seem suicidal and unlikely to happen. So I felt fairly secure while working as an American in the resistance camps. But on that afternoon on the border there was no denying the danger. We were dealing with very young, exhausted soldiers who only hours earlier had crossed out of a combat zone. Their command structure, nerves, and patience were seriously frayed. Many of the troops were trying to get wounded or sick comrades to the hospital.

As we struggled to get the aircraft ready to go, I found myself standing under the spinning rotors holding two large RPG-7 rounds (Soviet-made rocket-propelled grenades), one in each hand. The sick troopers we had decided to carry refused to leave their rifles behind—they had grown understandably attached to them, and they planned on using them in the future. One of the visiting AID Washingtonians was horrified by what he was seeing. Over the roar of the engine and the rotors, he reiterated the policy that prohibited our carrying "lethal material." I laughed as I told him to feel free to try to take the AK-47s away from the passengers. At that instant the bureaucrat saw the light. We took off (weapons and all) and the visitor never said another word about our blatant policy violation.

It seemed that almost every flight with Air Log provided a memorable incident. I once counted thirteen human beings crammed into the six-passenger helo—many of them were tiny Nicaraguan babies carried out by desperate mothers. On another trip we were carrying a wounded contra to the hospital. He had been peppered with shrapnel from a mortar round and was in great pain. The helo was overcrowded and I was doing my best to give him as much room as possible. As Roger reduced speed for landing, the door my back was jammed against popped open. Four hundred feet above the ground, I hung on for dear life. One day while taking off, we smashed through the top branches of a tree near the Strategic Command Headquarters LZ. I'm still not sure whether the pilot was unable to clear the tree or was just trying to shake up the rather smug Washington visitor we were carrying.

On a couple of occasions I got to use my military training by helping out with the "sling-loading" of fuel and supplies. It was very atypical work for a Foreign Service officer. A helicopter can carry extra cargo suspended from a hook. The sling carrying the cargo is attached to the hook by someone (me!) standing right beneath the hovering helicopter. Fun stuff!

As precarious as the helicopters were, they were safer than going overland. The route to Yamales from Tegucigalpa followed a series of increasingly bad—and dangerous—roads. The section from Tegucigalpa to Danli was a relatively easy highway trip. From there the paved roadway continued east into the Jamastran Valley. From Jamastran, a bumpy dirt road led to the village of Cifuentes. There things got really interesting.

The road from Cifuentes to the larger town of Las Trojes is almost indistinguishable from the Honduran-Nicaraguan border. One rather sensationalist magazine article dubbed it "the most dangerous road in the world." I think that was an exaggeration, but in June 1983, Dial Torgerson of the *Los Angeles Times* and freelance journalist Richard Cross had been killed there, either by a mine or by a rocket-propelled grenade. In January 1984 the Sandinistas killed U.S. Army pilot Jeffrey Schwab after he landed his helicopter on the road near Cifuentes. What sticks in my mind about that road was the fact that the Honduran army's border outposts overlooked both the road and the border that lay just beyond it, so anyone using it had to drive between the border and the Honduran machine guns.

On one trip down the road, I was escorting a visiting American (a private citizen) out to Yamales. For a variety of bureaucratic reasons we couldn't take her out on the helicopter, so I requested an embassy four-wheel-drive vehicle, stipulating that the driver had to be prepared for an overnight trip. Not having had time to obtain the required Honduran documentation for travel in the border zone, I had to summon all of my experience to finagle us through the checkpoints. When we stopped at the Honduran army brigade headquarters in the Jamastran Valley, I tried to evoke the image of a mysterious gringo official. I murmured to the duty officer that I was "from the *embajada* on a special mission." I flashed every official-looking ID card I had, and identified myself as Captain Meara (I was a reserve captain and had my reserve ID card with me). I must have created the appropriate image, because we were soon on our way with a letter that would get us through the checkpoints.

I had not explained our ultimate destination to the embassy driver (he was a Honduran employee more accustomed to the routine task of hauling embassy personnel to and from the Tegucigalpa airport). As we got closer and closer to contra-land he must have begun to realize where he was going. The poor fellow was nervous when he finally found himself at dusk in the midst of the heavily armed contras of the Yamales Strategic Command Headquarters. I arranged for him to have dinner and a place to sleep, and he was none the worse for his brief exposure to the Nicaraguan civil war.

The air transportation schedule to and from the Yamales Valley was very haphazard—the pilots were the best in the world, but the weather and a never-ending series of emergencies often caused last-minute changes in flight plans. If Bruce or Roger landed at a contra base camp and found a badly wounded trooper, that day's plan was immediately scrapped and an emergency medevac flown instead. Because we didn't have any communication between the valley and Tegucigalpa (we could have passed a message through the contra radio system, but I preferred not to use this means), I had to rely on the tentative plans of the pilots to arrange pickup times for my extractions from the valley. In other words, the pilots would drop me off and I would ask them to come back for me in two or three days. The slapdash planning occasionally left me stranded in the valley. This resulted in a bizarre little adventure unusual for a Foreign Service officer but very typical of the last phases of the contra war: a hitchhiking trip from Yamales to Tegucigalpa.

After three rainy days in the valley, I was ready to go home to Tegoose. Unfortunately, the helicopter arrived earlier than expected and I wasn't in position on the landing zone. After the chopper flew away, the cloud cover built up and I concluded that my ride probably wasn't going to be coming back that day. Hoisting my backpack, I set out for "Main Street Yamales" in search of alternate transportation.

I located a truck that had been carrying food to the troops, and the driver agreed to carry me as far as Danli. On the road from Capire to Trojes we got stuck in the mud twice and had to dig the truck out with shovels. Outside Trojes, we came upon another truck that had broken down. We stopped to help and learned that this truck was going all the way to Tegoose. What luck! I wouldn't have to search in Danli for a bus to Tegucigalpa. My jungle boots and large military rucksack might have raised a few eyebrows in the Danli bus station, but I'd figured Danli was probably used to such sights by then. I transferred my gear to the Tegucigalpa-bound truck and was homeward bound.

The drivers were Honduran campesinos who had upgraded to the ranks of truck drivers. They were great guys, salt-of-the-earth people who would do anything to help, but they weren't much for conversation on the six-hour trip. Their main worry was not the Sandinistas; they were much more concerned about hitchhiking Honduran soldiers, who were known to let off a few pot-shots if a driver didn't stop. Not wishing to test the soldiers' marksmanship, we courteously picked up every hitchhiker carrying a rifle. Like the drivers, these Honduran privates weren't scintillating raconteurs, but shortly before dusk we picked up another hitchhiker who spiced up the chatter considerably.

The hitchhiker was obviously not a campesino: he had a city slicker hair-cut and wore tight, uncomfortable designer jeans that no campesino would have put up with. Who was this person hitchhiking at dusk along the "most dangerous road in the world"? Of course! I should have guessed! He was an accountant from the firm of Price Waterhouse. He was working under contract for USAID as one of the many bean counters keeping a watchful eye on the contras. I remember thinking, "Only in Honduras! Only in the contra war!" We spent the rest of the trip talking about the fascinating challenges of being an auditor on the contra account. Soon the lights of Tegucigalpa appeared and my rainy weekend in the field was over.

CHAPTER 10

PRISONERS

High on a hillside, the trucks are loading
Everything's ready to roll.

This ain't no party, this ain't no disco,
this ain't no fooling around.

—From "Life During Wartime"
by the Talking Heads, 1979

ABOUT MIDWAY THROUGH MY TOUR IN HONDURAS, we started hearing ominous rumors about Sandinistas who were being held prisoner by the contras at a remote jungle site in the Bocay. According to the stories, the prisoners were in appalling physical condition, emaciated and sick. This was very disturbing news, and I was immediately dispatched to investigate. Giving no advance notice to the resistance, I arranged for the helicopter to drop me at the nearest available landing zone. There I met Comandante Wilfredo and explained to him that I wanted to visit the prison. Wilfredo quickly assigned one of his men to escort me to the prison site. He told the man that I would have no trouble in the jungle because I was "a military man."

My escort was a very big, very long-legged young contra. He was outfitted with standard jungle combat gear and carried the prized and feared FN/FAL, a Belgian-made assault rifle. I soon discovered that, like soldiers everywhere, my guide took pride in his ability to move quickly through his turf. I suspected that he was going to politely put the American "military man" through his paces.

The prison was only about a mile away from the landing pad, but in mountainous jungle a mile can be a long walk. My guide decided to use the shallow rivers of the area as a shortcut. Slogging hip-deep through the cool, clear river water, with three levels of bright green jungle foliage forming a translucent canopy overhead, I struggled to keep up with the contra and thought about how lucky I was to be there rather than in some mind-numbing embassy meeting. I was breathing heavily by the time we got to the prison. Entry into the camp involved climbing up muddy paths that at times became nearly vertical.

A colleague once described the Bocay as "like the mountains of Cambodia" (he had been there). My mental images of Cambodia come from the movie *Apocalypse Now*; it seemed to me that Colonel Kurtz would not have been at all out of place in that Bocay prison camp.

The contras had brought order to the jungle chaos. I found the prison compound to be as neat, orderly, and military as they could make it. Small buildings had been constructed from locally produced lumber. (The contras had converted their handheld chain saws into improvised saw mills.) Pathways led to the various sections of the camp. Sentries were at their posts, and the camp was firmly under the control of the commander of the resistance's military police unit.

I told the commander that I wanted to see the Sandinista prisoners, and he immediately took me to their compound. In a small, heavily guarded area surrounded by sentries and barbed wire, I found the group of supposedly emaciated POWs. The contra commander ordered a formation and the prisoners quickly formed up in military ranks. Many couldn't help breaking military discipline to gawk at the mysterious foreign visitor. Life at the prison must have been excruciatingly boring; my arrival was obviously the event of the year.

I made a head-count and took pictures of the group. Far from being emaciated, some of them actually seemed a bit plump. I randomly selected four prisoners from the formation and asked the commander for the opportunity to interview them. I was mostly interested in their health. While they were understandably unhappy about their detention, I found no evidence of starvation. Realizing that these prisoners would probably soon be released and returned to Nicaragua, I was careful about what I said to them. When one of the prisoners started to ask me questions about myself, I couldn't resist using a brusque line that seemed right out of the movies: "Look, I'm the one asking the questions here!" I concluded that the rumors of prisoners being emaciated and in grave danger were unfounded, and returned to the embassy.

For my report on the matter I needed the photos of the prisoners, and I needed them fast. So I took my film to a one-hour photo shop in downtown Tegucigalpa. Unfortunately, the shop had one of those automatic film-developing machines situated in a way that allows passersby to see the prints rolling out of the machine. I used a fake name when I filled out the form, and when my roll was coming through the development process I positioned myself so as to block the view of any curious window shoppers. That worked fine, but the young man who was operating the machine couldn't help but notice that my roll of film did not contain the usual tourist pictures or baby photos. As I paid the bill, he asked about the pictures.

The issue of Nicaraguan prisoners in Honduras was a hot topic in the newspapers at that time. I told him that I was a journalist and that the pictures had been taken in rebel camps in Colombia. "¡Que barbaridad!" (Such barbarity!), he replied. While watching the developing process I had made sure that only one set of prints was made; as we chatted about the tragic war in Colombia, I made sure I got all the negatives.

Everybody concerned wanted the prisoners to be sent home. They were a burden for the contras, who were forced to keep a military police company stationed in the inhospitable Bocay. The Nicaraguan prisoners also exposed the resistance to international criticism and created potential problems with the Hondurans. Soon we were working out the mechanics of a release. Before they could be repatriated, the prisoners had to be taken out of the jungle and moved closer to civilization. There were no roads to the Bocay, so we would have to use helicopters to carry them out.

We got permission from Washington to use the two Air Log choppers, and the contras prepared a holding facility in the much more accessible Yamales Valley. Hoping for a Christmas release, in early December 1988 we planned the details of the prisoner airlift. It was decided that a newly arrived colleague and I would be charged with supervising the move. I went out to the Bocay prison, and my partner went to the holding facility in Yamales. The pilots (Bruce and Roger) would shuttle between the two sites carrying small groups of prisoners.

On the day of the transfer I sat on a hilltop surrounded by triple-canopy jungle in the company of the quiet contra campesinos and their Sandinista captives. The prisoners stood in neat lines, blindfolded, with hands bound behind them. Periodically my radio sputtered and a little blue helicopter clattered into view. We would load a group of prisoners onto the chopper and off they would go to Yamales. At the other end, my colleague (who had been in Honduras for all of about ten days) oversaw the off-loading.

Within a few weeks the final release arrangements were worked out, and all of the prisoners were sent back to Nicaragua.

CHAPTER 11

THE WOUNDED

Someday you'll return to
Your valleys and your farms . . .
And you'll no longer burn
To be brothers in arms.

> —From the album *Brothers in Arms*
> by Dire Straits, 1985

MY FIRST REAL CONTACT WITH THE WORLD OF THE CONTRAS came a few months before I was deputized into the Special Liaison Office (SLO). One afternoon shortly after arriving at Embassy Tegucigalpa, I was seated at my desk in the ambassador's office. A call came through from Miami, and someone routed it to me. A Cuban-American doctor who had been doing volunteer work with wounded contras was looking for high-level embassy assistance in securing travel documents for a nineteen-year-old freedom fighter with a serious wound.

Maybe it was because I first learned Spanish in a Catholic missionary environment, or maybe it was the doctor's unfamiliar Cuban-accented Spanish or the long-distance telephone line; whatever the reason, I didn't understand the nature of the wound that we were discussing. It didn't really matter at the time. My military instincts kicked in and I promised the doctor that we would get the documents needed to get the wounded contra to Miami.

I put the case into the able hands of Wanda, the SLO's capable secretary. She was familiar with the procedures, and I knew that she wouldn't let the matter fall through the cracks. She was the wife of a military officer, and she reacted to wounded soldiers in much the same way that I did. Together we pushed the necessary paperwork through the embassy, and in record time we had the documents necessary to send the trooper to the hospital.

In the meantime, Wanda had spoken with the Cuban-American doctor. After we received word that the patient was "wheels up" en route to Miami, we talked about the case and Wanda filled in the gaps in my medical/anatomical Spanish. The young soldier's injuries included a serious wound in the penis. Every man in the room cringed at the thought of it.

The film industry and the news media present us with sanitized versions of war. Much of the ugliness is edited out. Wounds are neat and clean, and are often remedied by a bandage or, at most, an arm sling: John Wayne gallantly takes a bullet in the shoulder and courageously fights on. But real war wounds are very different. They are ugly. Unlike the Hollywood version of war injuries, wounds like the one we dealt with that day in Tegucigalpa take the mystique out of warfare and reduce it to the ugly, painful mess that it really is. Our work with the resistance put us in frequent contact with war's ugly consequences.

In the Yamales Valley, resistance medical doctors operated a clinic that served upward of ten thousand people. The two or three contra doctors who were usually on duty in Yamales were intermittently augmented by physicians contracted by USAID. Stretched out on army cots in a rudimentary wooden building with a dirt floor, gunshot wound victims were interspersed with malaria cases and women who had just given birth. I once started talking to one of the uniformed patients, assuming that he was a contra, and discovered that he was a Honduran soldier from the detachment stationed in the valley. The ERN doctors were doing a favor for the Honduran commander. In a similar spirit they treated many Honduran civilians. We once evacuated by helicopter a tiny, almost skeletal infant suffering from dehydration. Her claim to Nicaraguan nationality was doubtful, but because we were authorized to provide treatment only to Nicaraguans, we made her an honorary Nicaraguan. Some rules are made to be broken.

The Yamales medical facility eventually became known as "Clínica Doctor Javier." Bearded and about thirty years old, Javier looked a lot like the 1959 version of Fidel Castro. During our first meeting, he reclined in a hammock in his small shack next to the clinic. His AK-47 hung from a nail (he was not a pacifist). Bandages on his arms covered patches of mountain leprosy that he had picked up while in the field with contra combat units. As he would do with decreasing levels of personal invective during the months ahead, Javier opened our first conversation with a tirade about the vacillating U.S. support.

Before joining the resistance Javier had been the head of the intensive care unit at a hospital in Managua. Over the years he grew impatient with Sandinista tyranny and stupidity. He reached the breaking point when, during preparations for the long-awaited U.S. invasion, the Sandinistas ordered his intensive care patients out of the hospital as part of an invasion drill. People died. Javier joined the contras.

Javier and his medical colleagues were the most educated members of the resistance organization. Although they never took on high-level leadership positions, they were respected and listened-to members of the commanders' council. I admired them. Some came from that elite element of Nicaraguan society that had largely avoided the war. The doctors didn't have to be in Yamales. Like the campesinos they cared for, they were there because they were patriots.

The Nicaraguan war churned out platoons of permanently disabled young men. The number of crippled soldiers was kept low by the sad fact that only a small portion of the wounded lived through the evacuation; it was a long march from Chontales to Honduras, and there were no helicopters swooping in to take wounded contras to the hospital. Many of those who did survive eventually ended up at a place on the outskirts of Tegucigalpa called Rancho Grande, where, in a group of old farmhouses, the RN had established its rehabilitation center. The one hundred or so residents were mostly lower-leg amputees. There were a few paraplegics and a few people with serious head wounds. Like veterans' hospitals in the United States, Rancho Grande was a good place to discard romantic notions about war; it was a place to face war's ugly consequences.

The patients at Rancho Grande did their best to keep busy and to rehabilitate themselves. They set up a small shoe factory. Many took typing classes in hope of returning to duty in administrative jobs. A couple of disabled entrepreneurs set up a small "contra cross" factory and were soon turning M-16 bullets into the crucifixes that symbolized their anti-Communist rebellion.

Because of its proximity to Tegucigalpa, SLO personnel visited Rancho Grande quite often. I got to know many of the patients and was always amazed by their spirit. Even in the darkest days of 1989, when the RN's future looked very bleak, these young people who had sacrificed their health for the cause never gave up hope of victory.

Jehu, who took his war name from the Old Testament, was about twenty-two years old and was confined to a wheelchair after receiving a bullet wound near his spine. Nicaragua is known in Central America as the land of poets—even the humblest campesinos try to emulate the great Nicaraguan poet Rubén Darío. In this tradition, Jehu spun out verse expressing his thoughts on the war. He also did woodwork and carvings—one of his works depicted an eagle (the United States) sweeping down to break the red-and-black (Sandinista) chains that held down a poor Nicaraguan campesino.

Jehu's legs were not completely paralyzed, and his wounds had not left him incapable of having children. His wife and baby daughter lived with him in a curtained-off corner of Rancho Grande's paraplegic ward. The baby was named Ruth. Jehu explained that in the Bible, Ruth had lived in exile. So did his daughter.

American visitors to the embassy frequently asked for an opportunity to "meet some contras." Since Rancho Grande was close to Tegucigalpa, we ferried a lot of delegations out there to visit the wounded. Most of these visits went very well; sometimes they didn't.

The best visits occurred when former Nevada governor Mike O'Callaghan was in town. O'Callaghan is a big-hearted bear of a man who carries the scars of two wars. He lost a leg in combat in Korea. The contras loved it when he sat down with them and compared notes on the problems that come with this kind of wound. It was an honor and a pleasure to translate for the governor. Jehu asked O'Callaghan for help in getting some advanced medical treatment. A few weeks later, the governor returned to Honduras (as always, at his own expense) with Nevada's best neurosurgeon. The doctor worked on Jehu and other patients who needed his expertise.

The worst visits did not necessarily involve people who opposed U.S. aid to the contras. Those people usually avoided any contact with the human face of the resistance, and those who did come into contact with resistance troops usually didn't create a scene. For me, the worst visits were those of supposedly sympathetic Americans who—for a variety of reasons—just could not comprehend the situation of the Nicaraguan resistance.

Once, for example, a group of U.S. executives from companies that did business with the Defense Department came through Tegucigalpa on some sort of junket and asked to see contras. We had been asked to be hospitable and helpful, so we took these American businessmen on a bus trip to Rancho Grande. I gave them a little briefing on the way out to the site. On arrival, they filed off the bus like tourists in Disneyland and wandered around snapping pictures. The few embassy officers present helped with the translations. I shepherded a small group over to talk to Jehu and translated for about an hour. Jehu gave one of the visitors the eagle woodcarving I described earlier.

As we got back on the bus I thought everything had gone rather well, but during the ride back I started to wonder. "Why are they so damn dirty? Why can't they fix that place up?" complained one grumpy old man. I wondered if the color of their skin contributed to his condescension.

That night at the ambassador's residence, one of the people for whom I had translated congratulated me for having done such a good job. I started to accept his praise for the translation, but he interrupted and—referring to Jehu—said, "No, no, no. Not the translation. How long did it take you to put those words in that young man's mouth? How long did it take you to set that up?"

Taken aback by his question, I told the man that I took offense at his thinking that I would deliberately deceive him. (Privately, I was amazed at his conceit and self-importance. Apparently he thought himself worthy of some sort of elaborate deception operation.) It quickly became apparent that he and the other U.S. businessmen could not believe that young Nicaraguans were capable of the kind of devotion exhibited by Jehu and his brothers in arms. Maybe it was because many of these visitors had children who were Jehu's age; perhaps they knew that their spoiled kids could never have been so noble.

CHAPTER 12
VISITING THE TROOPS

¡Viva Nicaragua Libre!
¡VIVA!

EMBASSY TEGUCIGALPA RECEIVED A GREAT MANY OFFICIAL VISITORS. We frequently hosted congressional delegations (CODELs) made up of senators, representatives, and congressional staffers interested in the contra situation. The CODELs almost invariably asked to be taken out to see the contras. These requests placed some unusual demands on those of us engaged in contra liaison. My responsibilities as aide to the ambassador also came into play.

By this point in the conflict the contras had become quite adept at meeting and greeting VIPs from the North. Nevertheless, if a CODEL visit to Yamales went badly, we in the embassy—not the contras—would be held responsible. The wrath of the visitors would be especially severe if they were opposed to support for the Nicaraguan resistance. These people would automatically attribute any slipup to an embassy attempt to "hide something." It was our duty to make sure that the visitors got to see what they had come to see. Several factors—including the contras' natural desire to put their best foot forward, our real need for the visits to go smoothly, and the logistical difficulties of visits to Yamales—frequently put us in the position of having to orchestrate operations on scales rivaling a Cecil B. DeMille spectacular.

A typical CODEL visit would go as follows. The embassy would get a tele-gram from Washington informing us that Senators X, Y, and Z and a number of their staffers were coming to Tegucigalpa for a two-day visit. On the morning of the second day they would want to go to Yamales to "visit with the troops and meet with resistance leaders." We would immediately communicate the details to the resistance officers so that they would be available on the morning in ques-tion. The RN leaders would begin to prepare for the VIPs' arrival, and we would draw up the complicated plans for the helicopter transportation of the CODEL and the ambassador. We usually needed several helicopters to ferry out every-one involved. Coordination was very important. My personal nightmare during this period involved three wet and hungry U.S. senators and a U.S. ambassador stranded overnight in the Yamales Valley. Thank God, it never happened.

On the morning of the visit, I would helicopter out to the valley two or three hours in advance of the visitors to make sure that everything was set. I worked for the ambassador, and it was my job to prevent him from being embarrassed by a poorly coordinated visit. Inevitably, I would find the RN in the final phases of their preparations. The multitudes would be gathering. Whenever we brought VIPs to the valley, the resistance brought out the troops. At this point it was easy for them to put five thousand to seven thousand com-batants in military formation on their main parade field. Banners welcoming the senators had been prepared. An honor guard with AK-47 rifles lined the path from the helicopter landing zone. Like any advance man, I would go through the planned sequence of events with the resistance leaders.

Then, armed with smoke grenades and a ground-to-air radio, I would move to the LZ to anxiously await the arrival of the visitors. I say anxiously because I had just put five thousand people into the hot sun, and it was my job to make sure they stayed there until the visitors arrived. The CODELs very often fell behind schedule due to some dalliance or whim, and the poor contras would have to stand in the sun until the VIPs arrived. Because communications with the capital were so poor, I was never free of the nagging worry that the visit had been canceled and the troops were standing there for nothing.

Sometimes interesting emergencies popped up at the last minute. Once I was handling the visit of a VIP who had specified that there be no journalists on the site during his visit to the valley. He wanted to speak candidly to the troops in a way that would have been impossible in the glare of the interna-tional media. The contras had agreed to this condition, but when I arrived in the valley I found a group of foreign journalists on the scene.

Disaster was about to strike. The VIP's helicopter was en route from Tegoose and due to arrive very soon. I had to work quickly. I grabbed the senior RN officer onsite and vigorously protested this violation of our agreement. We were standing on a big hill overlooking the parade ground; the journalists were down at the bottom of the hill taking pictures of the troops. The exasperated RN officer said that he had no transportation available to get the reporters off the site. Fortunately, the helicopter that had carried me out to the valley was still in the area, and I had radio contact with it. I called the pilot and told him to stand by. I then cut a deal with the RN officer: if he could persuade the journalists to leave, I could provide the transportation.

I have to admit that I took some dark pleasure in what ensued. The contra officer used his walkie-talkie to speak to his subordinates on the parade ground. I watched the reporters gather up their stuff and move to the LZ. I called in the helicopter with my radio, and within minutes the journalists were winging their way out of the area. Right after they departed I heard the VIP helo coming up the valley. I gave the pilot clearance to land at Yamales International. The visit went very smoothly.

In fact, all of the CODEL visits went smoothly. The senators would get off the choppers and would be escorted to the reviewing stand. Climbing to the top, they would see for the first time the size of the crowd they had just walked through. The five thousand or so troops formed a virtual sea of coffee brown faces and olive drab uniforms. A platoon of amputees would usually be situated next to the reviewing stand (lest anyone forget). The troops would sing the Nicaraguan national anthem. Resounding cries of "¡Viva Nicaragua Libre!" would echo off the walls of the valley. The senior RN officers would introduce the guests, who—depending on party affiliation and political persuasion—would make speeches with varying degrees of encouragement or gloom. We would translate. Afterward the visitors would mingle with the troops while walking to the tent in which they would meet with the commanders. After they had talked things over for an hour or so, I would call in the helos and we would bundle the senators off to Tegucigalpa. I would always breathe a sigh of relief as the choppers disappeared over the walls of contra valley. The troops would go back to their units a little "pumped up" by the show of interest from the North.

CHAPTER 13

PICKING AT SCABS

Soon you learn the native customs,
soon a word of Spanish or two . . .
You know that you cannot trust them,
'Cause they know they can't trust you.

—From the song "Changes in Latitudes,
Changes in Attitudes" by Jimmy Buffett, 1977

ON THE NIGHT THAT GEORGE H. W. BUSH WAS ELECTED, while the rest of the U.S. embassy staff were with the Honduran elite at a big "Watch the Returns" party in Tegucigalpa, a colleague and I threw our own election-night party at Strategic Command Headquarters in Yamales. I bought five cases of warm soda and some potato chips, and distributed to our guests some Bush and Dukakis campaign buttons from the embassy's Public Affairs Office. The resistance had set up their own version of "campaign headquarters": two men hunched over shortwave radios keeping track of the electoral vote count as reported by Voice of America. I made a little speech explaining to the gathered troops that it was an American diplomatic tradition to have a party on the night of our national elections and to invite our friends to watch the results with us.

The contras had high hopes for the newly elected Bush administration, but their hopes were quickly dashed. To say that the first few months of the new administration were a disappointment would be a serious understatement. With the Soviet threat receding and bipartisanship the order of the day in Washington, the emphasis shifted away from efforts to keep the contras alive. The new priority was placating the critics in Congress who had been trying to scuttle the resistance. Columnist George Will assessed the new policy in the May 22, 1989, issue of *Newsweek*: "In practice bipartisanship buys popularity by adopting Democratic policies as in the liquidation of the contras."

On the ground, the new policy of bipartisanship quickly changed our approach to the resistance. While earlier we had been doing whatever we could to help them, now we were harassing them, "picking at their scabs," as one embassy officer put it. Human rights quickly became the instrument of choice in this campaign. Desperate to placate congressional critics of the resistance, and to keep their careers on track, Washington bureaucrats soon had us carrying out an absurd human rights inquisition in the Yamales Valley.

It seemed to me that the congressional critics we were trying so hard to please were not genuinely concerned about human rights; they were just using that issue as a device to dismantle the resistance. Under the new policy of bipartisanship, we replaced common sense and practicality with a legalistic approach that seemed designed to damage the resistance.

This new "pick at their scabs" policy is best illustrated by our reaction to a murder in the Yamales Valley. When a low-level commander became psychotic and killed one of his troops, the bureaucrats swung into action. Gone were the Reagan administration political appointees who had kept the anti-contra proclivities of the bureaucracy under control. Instead of treating this as a murder and letting the resistance's rudimentary criminal justice system handle it, Washington declared the incident a "human rights violation." Teams of lawyers swooped down from the United States. Not only was the murderer under investigation, but because this had been declared a human rights violation, an investigation was launched of the entire contra military chain of command (all the way to the top). The lawyers wanted to determine if the commanders had responded appropriately to the "human rights violation." If not, said Washington, they should all be dismissed. This represented a radical shift. We had very quickly moved from doing everything possible to help the contras stick together to looking for legal excuses to tear them apart.

I found myself ordered to explain obscure legal terms (*prima facie evidence*, for example) to campesino commanders who hadn't reached second grade. It was absurd, embarrassing, and thoroughly counterproductive. But we did our best to enforce the policy and never once even hinted to the contras that the messages we were delivering did not have our full personal support.

The contras were not blind to the hypocrisy of our new policy. It quickly became obvious to them that many of the people in the U.S. Congress who were attacking them on human rights issues were the very same people who had been steadfastly trying to engineer their destruction—the same people who were strangely silent on well-documented Sandinista human rights violations. Many in the resistance began to see "human rights" as just another Sandinista political device that was being used to effect their destruction. I found many of these congressional critics disingenuous; riding the coattails of human rights, they feigned moral outrage while actually seeking the destruction of the resistance army. Our ability to protect human rights was actually diminished by this political charade.

Other moves by the administration made our relationship with the resistance even more difficult. As a result of international agreements, and as part of the bipartisan accord with Congress, Secretary of State James Baker agreed that the resistance would not engage in "offensive actions." This agreement exposed the contras to a new avenue of attack: Sandinista charges that the contras were taking offensive actions inside Nicaragua could threaten U.S. humanitarian assistance to the resistance. We were soon telling the resistance, in effect, to be very careful not to shoot first in their contacts with the Sandinistas. After denying the contras lethal assistance and putting them in the position of having to return to Nicaragua with suicidally low quantities of ammunition, I found it particularly repugnant and despicable that we should now be haranguing them about the conditions under which our Congress would permit them to fire their weapons.

And through it all there was USAID. I see Congress's selection of the U.S. Agency for International Development to administer the humanitarian assistance program as a cruel and shameful move. It obligated the proud contras to kowtow to a seemingly endless stream of auditors, accountants, and bureaucrats. AID must have been horrified when, in the wake of the Iran-contra scandal, they were given responsibility for providing "humanitarian assistance" to the contras. They reacted in a cautious and bureaucratic manner. The first priority was to acquire the kind of oversight that would prevent any hint that the agency was engaged in any unsavory activity. They lined up three oversight organizations: the American firm of Price Waterhouse was contracted to do the accounting (literally bean counting); the Catholic Church was asked to help ensure that nothing lethal was mixed with the AID food;[1] and the AID Inspector General's Office watched the watchers.

If Congress's intent in selecting USAID was to prevent the resistance from continuing as a viable military organization, it could not have picked a better agency for the job. It seemed to me that some of the USAID people charged with administering the program yearned to turn the resistance into a pack of supine and easy-to-manage refugees. Fortunately (but not surprisingly), the contras proved to be stronger than their bureaucratic benefactors.

Difficult Meetings

During this period I often had to track down senior resistance leaders and arrange meetings to deliver tough messages from Washington. One very memorable one-on-one confrontation took place on Easter Sunday 1989 in a hotel room in Danli, Honduras. I had to tell Comandante Franklyn that unless a number of his staff officers were dismissed, we would cut off humanitarian assistance (i.e., their food supply). Happy Easter, Franklyn!

Difficult meetings like that one were common. Some did lead to the resignations of senior resistance military leaders. Although I won't go into the details of the substance (it was not related to the human rights problem discussed above), I can describe the atmosphere of one other particularly difficult encounter.

The instructions arrived in a cable from Washington. Immediate action was called for. I was the only one available who knew this resistance commander, so I was selected to deliver the message. It took a long time to get in touch with him. I thought he might be afraid of us; some people speculated that he might even have thought that we were setting him up for an ambush. We finally arranged to meet him in a house in Tegucigalpa. I was to go alone. Someone in the embassy raised an objection to this, saying that a one-on-one meeting might be dangerous. I thought he was talking about physical danger and said quite seriously that I didn't think that my contact would shoot me. There were chuckles as my colleague said that he was referring to the bureaucratic danger of not having a witness. Ah, the special concerns that arise when conducting diplomatic relations with armed insurgents!

I drove to the meeting site in my own car. On the way there I thought about what I had to say and how I was going to say it. I was still wearing my suit and tie. I didn't change into the less formal attire I usually wore when working with the contras because I wanted him to know that this visit was very official. After a friendly greeting we got down to business.

He had already guessed correctly the subject of my visit, and he accepted my message without anger or argument. I went over all of the required points and made sure that he understood all of them. He wanted us to understand his position, too, and explained it at length. He also asked about attitudes toward him in the embassy. Was there a vindictive feeling? Was there rancor? Were people out to get him?

There was none of that, and I felt it would be helpful if he knew it, so I slipped into the vernacular—the Nicaraguan slang I had learned in the base camps. "No, no," I answered in Spanish, "there is no personal rancor against you. I have been in all the meetings and nobody has been saying, 'Let's screw this guy!'" My use of the obscene slang not only presented him with a very clear answer to his question, it really broke the tension. He laughed out loud and said, "Man you sound just like one of us!" So, in the end, I *was* cursing like a contra.

Witchcraft

As part of our new "picking at scabs" human rights campaign, the State Department decided that the contras needed to be scolded not just by embassy staffers, but by a special emissary flown in from Washington. After arriving in Yamales, the visitor addressed a big meeting of all the resistance commanders. He began by trying to explain the rather arcane and legalistic Washington concerns about the way the contras had handled the "human rights" murder case. The term *prima facie evidence* was used yet again. After the scolding was concluded, we held a follow-up meeting with a smaller group of the most senior resistance military officials. A couple of men from the Political Directorate in Miami had flown in (just for the day, of course), and they were also present at the follow-up meeting.

The smaller meeting went well at first; both sides were letting their hair down, venting frustrations, and providing more candid background information than could have been shared in the larger forum. Our man talked about concerns on Capitol Hill, and the contras talked about the control and discipline problems of their thoroughly nonprofessional army. Mutual understanding was being improved and everything was going quite smoothly . . . until the contras started talking about one of their "special problems."

I'll never forget it. It was one of those moments in which something fundamental and important suddenly becomes very clear.

Speaking directly to the Washington visitor, Comandante Franklyn blurted it out, without hesitation or reluctance: "And you know that one of our biggest problems is that the Sandinistas have trained a large number of witches to come here and put spells on us."

The senior U.S. visitor issued a belly laugh, then slowly stopped laughing as the contra commanders remained stone-faced. The visiting Miami politicos fidgeted nervously. "You're putting me on, right?" asked the visitor. He tried to elicit laughter again, but again he was the only one laughing.

"No," said Franklyn, "we're quite serious. Just last week, a trooper in one of the regional commands almost died because of a hex put on him by the Sandinista witches. Their spells cause small animals to grow within the stomachs of their victims. Julio, go get the samples."

I will admit that I, too, was stunned at this point. I had spent a lot of time with the contras and had heard occasional references to witchcraft, but I had been busy with other things and hadn't had time for amateur anthropology or parapsychology. We knew that the Miskito Indians had strong witchcraft beliefs and practices, but we had always thought the ERN-N a more sophisticated group. They ran computer systems and flew helicopters.[2] But they also believed in witchcraft. We had painted a veneer of technology and sophistication over them, but they were still Nicaraguan peasants. And Nicaraguan peasants believe in witchcraft.

Julio came in carrying a shoebox that he carefully placed on the table. From the gingerly manner in which he carried it one would have thought that he was holding powdered plutonium or anthrax dust.

Franklyn opened the box and took out a small vial. "This is one of the little animals. It was vomited up by one of our soldiers after he fell victim to the spell of a Sandinista witch!"

The Washington visitor, yet to grasp that these men were completely serious, giggled and elbowed the embarrassed Miami politico sitting next to him. I did understand that the contras were serious, and I wished the Washington visitor would sit still and shut up. They passed the little vial around the table, and each visitor took a turn closing one eye and peering into the bottle. Now, I don't believe in witchcraft, but I had recently seen the science fiction movie *Alien* (with its stomach-dwelling, face-sucking monsters), and I had spent almost a year successfully dodging hepatitis, mountain leprosy, and a variety of other diseases that haunted contra valley. When my turn came to grasp the bottle and bring it up to my eye, well . . . I admit it, I passed.

Back at the embassy, I briefed my appalled superiors on the incident. They instantly understood that this story could be used to prove that the contras were hopeless lunatics.[3] I shared their concern, but in my own mind the incident simply served as further proof of the real nature of the contra military leadership: the contra military commanders, like the troops they led, were campesinos.

This meeting starkly illustrated the enormous cultural gap that existed between the contras and us. We were presenting them with diplomatic demarches on prima facie evidence. They were presenting us with evil spirits called forth by Sandinista witches.

Epiphany on the Coco

During my last few months in Honduras, I was engaged in a personal debate about U.S. interests and the contras. As I watched the changes in the Soviet Union and Washington, I began to question the rationale for our continued support of the very problematic resistance. Viewed from the geopolitical perspective, a lot of the justification for our support was disappearing. We had bought into the resistance effort because the Sandinistas had joined the evil empire. In the kinder, gentler post–Cold War world, Nicaragua's importance to our national security had diminished considerably. I began to think that our national interests no longer required us to support the resistance. Maybe it was time to disengage.

Throughout my tour I had tried to adhere to the detached, Special Forces approach to the guerrilla movement. Evaluating the resistance purely in terms of their utility to our national security interests, I took secret pride in my willingness to act coldly in defense of those interests. I had seen other U.S. officers get caught up emotionally in the resistance movement and lose objectivity. I was certain that I would never fall into the same trap. I was prepared to accept that it might be time for us to walk away.

But then, on that rainy day at Banco Grande that I described at the beginning of this book, I had my epiphany on the Río Coco. Meeting those young contras on their way back into Nicaragua reminded me of the human, moral aspects of what we were doing. Here they were, the real contras: not some abstract geopolitical pawns, not a bunch of silly, fat politicians in Miami, but brave young people with rifles about to cross into Sandinista Nicaragua.

After that meeting, I returned to the embassy and wrote a very emotional cable about my day on the Coco. I deliberately gave it a very low classification and marked it for wide distribution in the embassy and in Washington— I wanted to share my epiphany with my colleagues. It must have been one of those "you had to be there" situations, because the cable got no reaction beyond some good-natured ribbing from political section officers who suggested that it could be used as the basis for a TV miniseries.

But it had been a very important event for me. My encounter on the Coco with those wide-eyed young warriors caused me to look beyond geopolitics and to consider other interests, interests that I had overlooked in my cold, hard-boiled calculation of "what's in it for us." In my sentimental cable I used the term *embattled farmers* to describe the people with whom I had spoken. I had never liked the "moral equivalent of the founding fathers" rhetoric that the Reagan team had used; I had not encountered any Jeffersons or (Benjamin) Franklins among the contra leaders. But on the banks of the Coco River I had found some embattled farmers who had a lot in common with the New Englanders who fired that famous shot heard round the world. And they reminded me of a few things.

When I talked to individual contra combatants and asked them what they thought about the United States, they usually responded in what seemed to be a very naive manner. After expressing admiration and affection for our country, they would always say that the United States should continue to support them because they were fighting for democracy. Sometimes they expressed frustration and incomprehension at our failure to continue lethal assistance. Lacking our "sophisticated" understanding of the world situation, they innocently asked, "Why doesn't the United States support us? We're fighting for democracy!" It was a good question; sometimes wisdom comes from the mouths of babes—or from the mouths of embattled farmers who haven't finished second grade.

The State Department orientation course I had taken prior to being sent overseas had included some classes about the basic principles of American foreign policy. One lecture dealt with American exceptionalism: the notion that America is different, exceptional. While other countries base their foreign policy solely on cold calculations of national interest, America's exceptionalism requires us to consider some additional factors: we stand up for some very important human values. If America is the leader of the free world, and if we are to be true to our heritage—if we are to remain exceptional—then an inclination to help people who are fighting for freedom should be part of our foreign policy. Sadly, in those early days of the Bush administration I saw little evidence of any such inclination.

With policy shifting and my tour coming to an end, I prepared to leave Honduras having come full circle in my ideas on U.S. support for the resistance. I started out thinking that we should support the contras because they were a palatable way for the United States to deal with the Sandinista-Soviet security threat. Glasnost and perestroika caused me to question the rationale for continued support. But I ended up believing that we should stick with the Nicaraguan resistance for spiritual and moral reasons, for reasons related to American exceptionalism and our national heritage. I ended up thinking that we should stick with them just because they really were freedom fighters.

In mid-June 1989 I went on my last reporting mission to the Yamales Valley. I had already received my transfer orders, but the chargé asked me to go out to Yamales to write one final series of analytical reports. After a few days spent rambling through the valley and talking to contras, I prepared to take my final leave of them. Throughout that last visit I had experienced a rather predictable sense of remorse and guilt. I felt that I was abandoning the resistance. Like all the other gringos who had come and gone before me, I was leaving; I was going to a better place. It was the rainy season, and I was literally leaving the resistance in the mud. I felt like a deserter.

With my helicopter en route from Tegucigalpa, the resistance commanders and I sat down for a going-away lunch. We joked quietly about some of the things that had gone on during the previous year, and we all spoke confidently about what we all knew to be a very uncertain future. They presented me with a certificate that declared me to be their brother . . . and a freedom fighter. I said I would try to tell their story to the outside world, to explain their struggle to the world beyond Yamales.

Mercifully, the sound of the approaching helicopter signaled an end to that painful and moving luncheon. I climbed into the chopper and flew out of the valley.

CHAPTER 14
CONTRARIAN CONCLUSIONS

In the world's broad field of battle,
In the bivouac of Life
Be not like dumb, driven cattle!
Be a hero in the strife.

—"Psalm of Life" by Henry Wadsworth Longfellow

ON NOVEMBER 10, 1989, FOUR MONTHS AFTER I LEFT CENTRAL AMERICA, I drove from my new home in Bilbao, Spain, to the U.S. Air Force base at Zaragoza. I was in search of a turkey for Thanksgiving dinner. As I cruised down Spain's beautiful Ebro Valley, I listened to the radio reports from Berlin. The wall was falling and the world was changing.

Within three months, the wave of political change that seemed to be sweeping the world reached Nicaragua—the Sandinistas were voted out of office. As I read the reports from Nicaragua, I thought back to conversations with contras in which we had joked bravely (and hopelessly) about meeting one day in "Free Managua." Suddenly such meetings seemed possible. For a time it had seemed that it wouldn't work out this way—for a time it seemed that Nicaragua would follow the example of Cuba and become an isolated vestige of Communism.

Watching developments from my new European home, I realized that I was probably one of very few people who saw any connection between the fall of the Berlin Wall and the contras. Many seemed to regard the war in Nicaragua as a squalid little affair with no real connection to the momentous events taking place in Europe. But I didn't see it that way. I think the contras knocked a few bricks off that wall in Berlin. They stood up against Communist efforts to put their little country on the evil side of the ideological divide, and they were loyal allies in our efforts to resist the expansion of that evil empire, that empire that the wall so perfectly symbolized.

I realize that my views on the contras are very unusual, but I had some very unusual vantage points on the Central American conflict, and I came away with a number of conclusions that run contrary to the conventional wisdom.

My positive sentiments about the Nicaraguan resistance put me very clearly in contrarian territory. It would be hard to exaggerate the extent to which the contras were vilified in the United States. Perhaps as a result of the bad image presented by the "Comandantes Less-Than-Zero" of the Directorate and the Iran-contra scandal, the left-leaning U.S. entertainment industry made the contras the ultimate bad guys. By the early 1990s contras frequently showed up in U.S. movies and TV programs as sinister drug dealers or bloodthirsty mercenaries; by the mid-'90s they were even being blamed for our crack cocaine epidemic.

But I think the world should be proud of the contras. The young peasants of Nicaragua refused to be enslaved by Communism. They waged a courageous struggle against great odds. They persevered when the situation looked very bleak. They sacrificed for the good of their people and for the future of their country. They were noble and honorable freedom fighters. The *mucos* refused to be like Longfellow's "dumb, driven cattle." They were heroes in the strife.

I give the contras most of the credit for the elections held in Nicaragua in February 1990. I believe the Sandinistas realized that the Bush administration was looking for an excuse to abandon the Nicaraguan resistance. I think the Communists were hoping that they could get through the election, watch the gringos walk away, and then continue with their totalitarian project. Sadly, it seemed that Washington was prepared to go along with this charade. I doubt the Sandinistas would even have held the elections if the contras had not still been in the field. But because the contras were still a threat, the Sandinistas took a chance. And they lost.

El Salvador also turned out to be a very clear Cold War victory for our side. During late 1991 and early 1992, the Salvadoran government and the FMLN reached agreements that ended the war. In the *New York Times Sunday Magazine* of February 9, 1992, journalist James Le Moyne summarized the conciliation: "In the end, while both sides made major concessions, it was the rebels who changed ideology. After years of spurning elections and demanding a direct share of power, they recognized the legitimacy of the government, accepted gradual disarmament, and pledged to enter elections as legitimate political parties."

In what is perhaps the best indication of the true human rights role played by American military advisers during the conflict, journalist Le Moyne pointed out that in the final phases of the Salvadoran peace negotiations, the rebels stated a desire for better relations with the United States: "They argue that only Washington can guarantee that the peace accord will be implemented, and that American military advisors are needed to keep the Salvadoran military in line." So I guess we were not the monsters they had made us out to be after all.

While we frequently stumbled and made some tactical mistakes, I think that Americans should be proud of what the Reagan administration did and tried to do in Central America. Whether you look at our efforts there as the pursuit of narrow national security interests or as a messianic campaign for human freedom (it actually had elements of both), our goals were noble and our methods honorable. And we achieved our successes without involving large U.S. military units. At the beginning of the decade there was a lot of concern that Central America might become America's next Vietnam. Because we succeeded, it did not turn out that way.

But I don't think that everyone has the right to feel good about their actions during the Central American conflict. I think those Americans who gave aid and comfort to the Sandinistas and the Salvadoran Communists should feel guilty. They were on the wrong side in the Cold War. Some of those people were knowingly supporting Communism, others were what Lenin called "useful idiots." All of them should feel remorse about supporting that evil system.

I think my journey through Central America provides some lessons about the challenges that arise when the United States tries to deal with insurgency and promote democracy on distant shores. The paragraphs on the following pages summarize my "lessons learned."

Cultural factors really are the equivalent of a terrain feature that cannot be ignored. I had my first perplexing encounters with cultural differences as a twenty-year-old in Guatemala. How could those nice people be so cruel to their Indian Cinderellas? Later, my counterinsurgency classroom in El Salvador provided more reminders that sometimes foreigners really don't think like we do. In the contra rehabilitation center I observed the inability of even sympathetic Americans to understand Nicaragua's wounded young contras. And then there was the memorable contra witchcraft meeting and all that it showed about the cultural divide that separates Americans from the world's peasant warriors.

Fluency in foreign languages is the indispensable key to understanding. Even with strong language skills it is difficult for us to really understand people like the contras; without those skills we have no chance of understanding. When working with insurgents, we don't need people like that fellow from Washington who wandered uncomfortably through the contra camp until he found the English-speaking politico from Miami, or the colonelcrat from Fort Bragg who seemed so proud of his inability to speak Vietnamese.

In order to be effective, you need to be able to sit in late-night clouds of cigarette smoke and coffee fumes and understand the anguished stories of peasant guerrillas. You need to know what people mean when they refer to you as a *chele*, and you definitely need to know the difference between *hablando* paja and *haciendo* paja! You need to be able to curse like a contra when necessary, and if you want to really understand them, you need to have a level of fluency that lets you feel the same goose bumps they feel when they sing that special song about those who have been lost. If you can't do these things, you run the risk of never understanding them, of never seeing them as real, complicated human beings. You will be prone to seeing them as monodimensional caricatures like the stereotyped characters of *Doonesbury*. Or as interchangeable LBGs. Or as disposable policy options.

Regional expertise and experience are crucial. People working on insurgencies shouldn't be doing so on their first trip to the region. In Yamales I found myself making use of lessons learned as far back as my student days in Guatemala. Insurgency is serious business, and amateurs should not be allowed to dabble in it.

Americans need to be aware of the institutional biases and shortcomings that make it difficult for us to deal with foreign insurgencies. We need to realize that our big, high-tech military machine—our big catapult—might not be much use against an insurgency built around people like Miguel Castellanos. I saw many signs of our weaknesses in this area: the tank traps we were building in the "Choluteca gap"; our big bucks, high-tech approach to support for the Salvadoran armed forces; our army's conviction that "any good officer" can work on insurgency. I came to the conclusion that our powerful military is a blunt instrument; it is very capable of performing its primary mission (destroying enemy military forces), but it is poorly suited for cross-cultural battles for foreign hearts and minds.

I saw broader institutional deficiencies in the disturbing contrasts between how the U.S. government helped "our" Central American insurgents and how the Communists helped theirs, between the careful preparation and guidance given by the Communists to Miguel Castellanos and the pathetic struggles of Comandante Franklyn to learn military history from supermarket paperbacks.

Regarding the benefits and perils of surrogate warfare, I think the fact that we avoided the use of large U.S. military units is the best demonstration of the advantage of this approach. As for the perils, I would simply point to the complexities that arise when you are dealing with people like some of those we dealt with in El Salvador. I think you have to go into a situation like this with your eyes open, realizing that none of the people you have to work with will be perfect, and some of them may be monsters.

Finally, when we get involved in foreign insurgencies, we should always strive to conduct ourselves in a manner consistent with our national values and with the requirements of American exceptionalism. We should remember our history. We should remember that we were helped by foreigners when we were fighting for our independence. We should remember that we too were once embattled farmers. When we decide to work with foreign forces in an insurgency, we should not think of these people as disposable pawns. They may come from another country and culture, they may be dark-skinned campesinos and not middle-class Americans, but their lives are no less valuable than ours. We should not be treacherous in our dealings with them. We should not be willing to contemplate "ballistic demobilization" or its policy equivalent.

The months following the fall of the Berlin Wall were a very strange and uneasy time for erstwhile Cold Warriors. The compass that had guided us for the previous forty-five years no longer worked. The conflict that had provided our mission and had justified our actions and policies simply disappeared. In winning the war we lost our cause.

I began to have doubts about the continued utility of a career in the government. Without the Cold War, without the opportunity to participate in the titanic struggle for world freedom . . . well, it just wasn't the same. The Cold War had allowed us to be American revolutionaries. It had allowed us to go to foreign countries to help in the battle against tyranny. While I was in Central

America I had worked to help stop the FMLN and later to overthrow the FSLN. In the post–Cold War environment, I found myself helping American companies sell their wares in the European market. It just wasn't the same. When I looked ahead to future assignments, where I had once seen opportunities for Cold War derring-do I now saw a relatively boring panorama of bureaucratic jobs.

Some Cold Warriors tried to grab onto the drug war as their next battle. Some seemed to itch for an opportunity to mix it up with such oddball misfits as Peru's Shining Path or the Philippines' New People's Army. The newspapers reported that intelligence agencies that had once worked against Karla's KGB were now preparing to steal business secrets from foreign industrial competitors. In the United States, there seemed to be a determined effort to use Japanese microchips as a psychological substitute for the Soviet missiles that had once provided such a unifying threat. Panama's Noriega very briefly served as the bogeyman. But it was all pathetic: the old warriors were clutching desperately at straws.

As difficult as it was to admit, the war was over. A new world had been born, but the victors were suffering from postpartum depression. Ironically, it was after the war that we suffered from the lack of purpose expressed in the question "What are we fighting for?" We weren't fighting anymore, and peace presented us with profound questions about national purpose. For those of us who had dedicated ourselves to national service these issues became questions of personal identity and purpose. In a world in which almost everyone embraces the values of Western democracy, would the United States cease being exceptional and become just another country bent on the protection of narrow national interests? Service to such a government would not be nearly as meaningful as it had been during the Cold War. We had been crusaders fighting in a holy war; we had been on a forty-five-year jihad against the Communist infidels. Peace and victory threatened to change us from crusaders to bureaucrats.

The Communists were gone.

Deep down, I already missed them.

ACKNOWLEDGMENTS

I WOULD LIKE TO THANK THE MANY PEOPLE who helped and encouraged me during the writing of this book.

The original idea for *Contra Cross* probably came from Ambassador Ted Briggs and his deputy at the American embassy in Tegucigalpa, John Penfold. Several times, after I briefed them on visits that I had made to the contra base camps, they paused and said, "You ought to write a book about this."

Several friends with significant experience in the region reviewed the manuscript and offered constructive criticism. My thanks in this regard to Ambassador Donald C. Johnson, Tim Brown, Raymond Dalland, and one friend whose name can't be mentioned.

I consider myself very fortunate to have been able to work with Mark Gatlin and the Naval Institute Press. Mark believed in this project from the start. Throughout the publication process he was a very thoughtful editor and an enthusiastic advocate. Thanks, Mark. Copy editor Melinda Conner did a wonderful job keeping the book on the straight and narrow, and offered very good advice. She also knew far better than I where to put all the Spanish accent marks. Thanks, Mindy.

I owe my introduction to Central America to the Christian Brothers of La Salle, and Manhattan College. I would like to express special thanks to my Spanish teacher, Brother Peter Stewart, and to the Catholic religious community of Huehuetenango, Guatemala.

I would also like to thank my brother, Edward Charles Meara. Long ago he gave me Longfellow's "Psalm of Life." It has always been my favorite poem. Thanks, Ed.

Finally, I would like to thank the countless Central Americans who showed me such wonderful kindness during my time in their region. It is my hope that this book will in some small way contribute to a deeper understanding of what happened in Central American during the 1980s. I also hope it will improve my country's understanding of its southern neighbors, and our ability to deal effectively with people from different cultures.

Of course, I bear full responsibility for the book. Any errors or omissions are mine alone.

NOTES

Preface

1. I was ending my stay in Honduras (my tour of duty had ended), but the embassy had asked me to accompany Franklyn to a meeting in Washington.

Chapter 1. Guatemala

1. Writing of the visitor's experience in Spain, John A. Crow, in his book *Spain: The Root and the Flower* (Berkeley: University of California Press, 1985), describes a phenomenon that I think applies to the way newly arrived Americans react to Central America: "The foreigner who enters Spain with heart and mind open begins immediately to enjoy the Spanish sun and the Spanish joy of living that transcends economic insecurity. The foreigner can accept these things freely because he feels no sense of responsibility about his environment. This feeling may last for several months, but at last he begins to sense the tremendous price that Spaniards have paid for their delicious anarchy, then the visitor is saddened. He feels the gnaw of frustration, the sharp threat of despair" (p. 367).

Chapter 3. In the Green Machine

1. To this day I am not sure whether the assignment was a deliberate decision or a bureaucratic error. I suspect the latter. At the time of my application for active duty, Special Forces officers carried the same occupational specialty code as foreign area specialists (code 48). I suspect the board saw that I was qualified as a 48 and mistakenly assumed that I was an area specialist.

2. Lt. William R. Meara, "Operation PBSUCCESS (Guatemala 1954): An Analysis of Long Term Impact on U.S. National Interest," analytical research paper submitted to the Foreign Area Officer Course of the JFK Special Warfare Center, November 1984.

3. See David Nolan, *The Ideology of the Sandinistas and the Nicaraguan Revolution* (Coral Gables, Fla.: Institute of Interamerican Studies, Graduate School of International Studies, University of Miami, 1984). Nolan went on to join the Foreign Service.

4. I was asked to sponsor two officers from the Philippines. One went on to play a fairly important role in the overthrow of the Marcos dictatorship. On the day of the revolt, the two classmates found themselves on opposing sides. I later learned that the friendship forged in the PSYOP course had allowed the two of them to communicate during the crisis and avoid some unnecessary bloodshed. So the PSYOP course wasn't a total waste of time.

5. Col. John D. Waghelstein, "Post-Vietnam Counterinsurgency Doctrine," *Military Review* (May 1985): 42–49.

Chapter 4. El Salvador

1. As it turned out, this rule had no real impact on my life because the girl I was hoping to meet was about fifteen hundred miles to the northeast, in Santo Domingo. I met Elisa in July 1992.

2. The "security forces" were the quasi-police, quasi-military forces that worked in El Salvador: the Treasury police, the National Guard, and so on. These forces were thought to be responsible for much of the human rights abuses. The military forces (army, air force, navy, etc.) were considered to be in a different category (but were not immune from charges of serious human rights violations).

3. Why fifty-five advisers? I heard the number was derived from the U.S. speed limit.

4. Waghelstein, "Post-Vietnam Counterinsurgency Doctrine." Waghelstein is quoting Ernest Evans, from *Rift and Revolution: The Central American Imbroglio*, ed. Howard Wiarda (Washington, D.C.: American Enterprise Institute for Public Policy Research, 1984), pp. 186–187.

5. Joaquin Villalobos, "El Estado actual de la guerra y sus perspectives" (The actual state of war and its outlook), *ECA—Estudios Centroamericanos* (published by Universidad Centroamericana José Simeón Cañas) (March 1986): 169–204; translations by William R. Meara.

6. Much of the information about Castellanos's background comes from the book *Conversaciones con el Comandante Miguel Castellanos*, by Javier Rojas U. (San Salvador: Editorial Adelante, 1986). Castellanos gave me an inscribed copy in May 1987.

Chapter 7. Embattled Farmers

1. For comparison: "Washington's army reached its first peak of strength with 18,000 in the summer of 1776. It fell to 5,000 by the end of the year, rose to a little more than 20,000 in mid-1778, and then declined." Douglas Southall Freeman, *George*

Washington, vol. 4, p. 622, as quoted in *Yankees at the Court*, by Susan Mary Alsop
(New York: Washington Square Press, 1982).

Chapter 9. Stairway to Heaven

1. Contras in the inaccessible Honduran Mosquitia and Bocay region were supplied
    through dangerous parachute drop operations flown by DC-3 and DC-6 aircraft con-
    tracted by USAID. On one very sad day one of these planes ran into bad weather while
    en route back to Toncontin; after repeatedly trying to fly around the bad weather, the
    plane ran out of fuel and crashed into a mountain outside Tegucigalpa, killing the
    pilots and the contra supply personnel.

Chapter 13. Picking at Scabs

1. This resulted in the perhaps apocryphal story of nuns running metal detectors over
    the first shipment of AID bananas (looking for banana clips, one joke claimed). I say
    apocryphal because it strikes me as being ridiculous and improbable, but a colleague
    claims that it really happened.

2. The contras used computers for a variety of applications; ironically, I became com-
    puter literate largely through my contact with them. Like many people, I had long
    recognized the need for a PC but knew nothing about them and was unsure of which
    brand to buy. When I saw the contras operating rugged Tandy PCs from rickety gen-
    erators inside tents that were alternately buffeted with monsoon-like rains and dry-
    season dust storms, I was sold on Tandy. When the computer boxes arrived from the
    United States, a young contra computer geek came to my house to install the hard disk
    that I wrote this book on.

3. I ask readers who would think condescendingly of contra witchcraft to consider some
    of the rights and rituals of our Christian churches. I'm a Catholic. We have incense
    and holy water and even exorcisms. We should also remember some of the incidents
    of our own early history; Salem, Massachusetts, comes to mind.

INDEX

Note: Page numbers followed by the letter *n*, plus a number, refer to endnotes. The author is referred to throughout the index simply as Meara.

ABOUT THE AUTHOR

THE SON OF A NEW YORK CITY POLICEMAN, William Meara studied international affairs and economics at Manhattan College. While a student, he worked as a volunteer English teacher at a Catholic mission school in Huehuetenango, Guatemala. As an army officer, he graduated from Ft. Bragg's Special Forces and Foreign Area Officer courses and served in Honduras, El Salvador, and Panama. In El Salvador, Bill was one of fifty-five American trainer/advisers assisting in the struggle against the Communist FMLN. After leaving the army, he joined the U.S. Foreign Services and was sent back to Honduras as special assistant to the U.S. ambassador, serving as one of the embassy's liason officers to the Nicaraguan Democratic Resistance (the contras). A career diplomat, Bill went on to serve in Spain's Basque country, in the Dominican Republic, and in the United Kingdom. From 2000–2003 he was principal officer and American consul in the Azores islands of Portugal.

He can be reached at bill.meara@gmail.com.

THE NAVAL INSTITUTE PRESS is the book-publishing arm of the U.S. Naval Institute, a private, nonprofit, membership society for sea service professionals and others who share an interest in naval and maritime affairs. Established in 1873 at the U.S. Naval Academy in Annapolis, Maryland, where its offices remain today, the Naval Institute has members worldwide.

Members of the Naval Institute support the education programs of the society and receive the influential monthly magazine *Proceedings* and discounts on fine nautical prints and on ship and aircraft photos. They also have access to the transcripts of the Institute's Oral History Program and get discounted admission to any of the Institute-sponsored seminars offered around the country.

The Naval Institute also publishes *Naval History* magazine. This colorful bimonthly is filled with entertaining and thought-provoking articles, first-person reminiscences, and dramatic art and photography. Members receive a discount on *Naval History* subscriptions.

The Naval Institute's book-publishing program, begun in 1898 with basic guides to naval practices, has broadened its scope to include books of more general interest. Now the Naval Institute Press publishes about seventy titles each year, ranging from how-to-books on boating and navigation to battle histories, biographies, ship and aircraft guides, and novels. Institute members receive significant discounts on the Press's more than eight hundred books in print.

Full-time students are eligible for special half-price membership rates. Life memberships are also available.

For a free catalog describing Naval Institute Press books currently available, and for further information about subscribing to *Naval History* magazine or about joining the U.S. Naval Institute, please write to:

Member Services
U.S. NAVAL INSTITUTE
291 Wood Road
Annapolis, MD 21402-5034
Telephone: (800) 233-8764
Fax: (410) 571-1703
Web address: www.navalinstitute.org